Student Solutions Manual
to accompany

QUALITY

Fifth Edition

Donna C. S. Summers
University of Dayton

Prentice Hall

Boston   Columbus   Indianapolis   New York   San Francisco   Upper Saddle River
Amsterdam   Cape Town   Dubai   London   Madrid   Milan   Munich   Paris   Montreal   Toronto
Delhi   Mexico City   Sao Paulo   Sydney   Hong Kong   Seoul   Singapore   Taipei   Tokyo

Vice President and Executive Editor: Vernon R. Anthony
Acquisitions Editor: David Ploskonka
Editorial Assistant: Nancy Kesterson
Director of Marketing: David Gesell
Senior Marketing Coordinator: Alicia Wozniak
Project Manager: Maren L. Miller
Senior Operations Supervisor: Pat Tonneman
Operations Specialist: Laura Weaver
Senior Art Director: Diane Y. Ernsberger
Cover Designer: Jason Moore
AV Project Manager: Janet Portisch
Printer/Binder: Demand Production Center
Cover Printer: Demand Production Center

Credits and acknowledgments borrowed from other sources and reproduced, with permission, in this textbook appear on appropriate page within text.

10 9 8 7 6 5 4 3 2 1

www.pearsonhighered.com

ISBN 10: 0-13-506720-0
ISBN 13: 978-0-13-506720-8

Contents

Chapter 1

1.2　Feigenbaum's definition is very comprehensive and focuses on the customer. Deming's definition of quality, 'non-faulty systems' appears to be narrow on the surface, however, to have a non-faulty system, the system must meet the expectations as identified by the customer(s), thus enabling us to link to Feigenbaum's definition. The definition presented by ASQ has several similarities to Feigenbaum's including quality as a subjective term, each person having their own definition of quality, ability to satisfy stated or implied needs and being free from deficiencies.

1.3　Customer determination: replacement muffler is new, not used, that it is needed.
Actual experience: does the muffler muffle? Service?
Requirements: Service at time of replacement? On time? As promised?
Technically operational: does the muffler fit the car?
Entirely subjective: cleanliness of shop? Courtesy of service people?

1.4　Clock: actual experience: what does the customer want or need from clock
　　　　Stated/unstated: tells time/decorative
　　　　Conscious/merely sensed: dimensions/nice face on clock
　　　　Technically operational/subjective: keeps time/sound of ticking
　　Grocery: actual experience: customer need for grocery
　　　　Stated/unstated: organic/wide variety
　　　　Conscious/merely sensed: type of food/five senses reaction to food
　　　　Technically operational/subjective: item availability/types of offerings
　　Doctor: actual experience: patient's actual experience at doctor's office
　　　　Stated/unstated: sterile equipment/clean environment/infection control and staff that cares about infection risk
　　　　Conscious/merely sensed: answers to questions/bedside manner
　　　　Technically operational/subjective: able to prescribe medicine/able to suggest lifestyle changes.

1.5　For example: Quality is defined by the customer's actual experience with the product or service. What did they think they wanted before the experience? What did they think after they interacted with the product or service? Did they feel they achieved value for their time and money? Productivity refers to the effectiveness with which things get accomplished, how well are resources used.

1.6　Customer determination: does the clean clothing meet the expectations of the customer?
Actual experience: Does the clothing feel, smell, look clean while wearing?
Requirements: clean, pressed clothing
Technically operational: clean, pressed, no damage
Entirely subjective: Does the clothing look, smell, feel good?

1.7　See Figure 1.3

1.8　Specification: A document that states the requirements to which a given product or service must conform.
Tolerances: the amount of variation allowed from a standard.

Inspection: Measuring, examining, testing, or gauging one or more characteristics of a product or service and comparing the results with specified requirements to determine whether conformity is achieved for each characteristic.
Prevention: Prevention refers to those activities designed to prevent non-conformances in products and services.

1.9   Inspection occurs after the fact, the product has been produced, the service has been provided. Quality control goes beyond inspection in that statistical records are kept, but again, this information is gathered after a problem has occurred. It is not a proactive method of ensuring the quality of a product or service. Statistical quality control expands on the concept and performs statistical analysis on the information gathered to determine whether or not improvements can be made to the product or service. It is only when a company practices statistical process control that the company focuses on being proactive in the face of quality issues. Information is used to improve the way a product is produced or a service is provided. In total quality management the proactive philosophy is expanded and applied to all areas of the company.

1.10   Inspection: Normally occurs at the completion of a product or service. The product or service is compared against a standard and judged as good or bad.
Quality Control: Firms practicing quality control review their products or services by comparing them with specifications. This information is used to design, produce, review, and improve the item's quality.
Statistical Quality Control: Practitioners use statistical date to analyze and solve problems.
Statistical Process Control: SPC focuses on process improvement in order to eliminate defects.
Total Quality Management: TQM focuses on achieving customer satisfaction through system and process improvement.
Continuous Improvement: Companies taking this approach are interested in improving systems and processes in order to continually provide value for their customers.

1.12   Example Specifications:

Item	Specification
Room Cleanliness	2 sets of clean towels
Room Cleanliness	Room vacuumed daily
Pool Cleanliness	No towels/debris around pool area
Pool Cleanliness	Correct Ph

1.13   Wanamaker treats bases quality on the customer's actual experience with the product or service (return the goods and get their money back). Wanamaker considers the customer's value determination which relates to Feigenbaum's customer's needs stated or unstated, conscious or merely sensed, technically operational or entirely subjective.

Chapter 2

2.1   The three purposes of Dr. Shewhart's control charts are: to define standards for the process, to aid in problem-solving efforts to attain the standards, and to serve to judge if the standards have been met. These three purposes work together during an integrated problem-solving process. The first purpose, defining standards, sets the expectations for the process. The third purpose, judging if the standards are met, is used to determine if the process is capable of meeting the expectations placed on it. If the process is not capable, then the second purpose, to aid in problem-solving efforts, comes into play as the charts are used to determine the root causes associated with the processes' inability to meet specifications.

2.2   Deming's fourteen points interact by creating an integrated and systematic method of approaching the management of an organization. This method is grounded in the philosophy of constantly and forever improving the business of providing goods and services. While the fourteen points do not tell a company how to run every aspect of its business, they do provide guidelines which support the development of company-specific management systems grounded in continuous improvement.

2.6   Little q has a focus on the product, manufacturing, and the person buying the product. Its focus is narrow. Big Q, on the other hand focuses on the products and services as well as any processes involving the customer. The customer is anyone who interacts with the product or service. Big Q requires a larger focus on how we do the work we do and what is involved in our business.

2.7   Juran's approach to quality is described by his Trilogy of quality: quality planning, quality control and quality improvement.

2.8   The steering arm sets direction, monitors progress, removes barriers and provides resources to those solving the problems (the diagnostic arm). The diagnostic arm carries out the steps of quality problem solving: investigation, root cause determination, propose potential solutions, implementation, and measurement of success.

2.9   A. Crosby's definition of quality: conformance to requirements
            B. Crosby's system of quality: prevention of defects
            C. Crosby's performance standard: zero defects
            D. Left to the reader.

2.10   Customer satisfaction centers on how the customer felt the last time he or she bought a product or service from an organization. It is a comparison between customer expectations and customer experience. A successful customer is one who receives a product or service that meets his or her expectations the first time. When a customer is merely satisfied, steps may have been taken to rework or redo the product or service until the customer is happy. In the action of satisfying a customer whose expectations weren't met the first time, the company may have incurred quality costs.

2.11 Crosby's erroneous assumptions:
Quality is goodness, luxury.
Quality is the responsibility of the quality control department.
Quality is intangible and not measurable.
Quality problems begin with the operator.
There is an "economics of Quality."

2.12 Dr. Deming: Constancy of purpose/Continuous improvement/Institute training
Dr. Juran: Quality Improvement/Steering arm provides resources for improvement/Big Q
Crosby: Economics of Quality/prevention of defects.

2.13 Taguchi's loss function describes the difference between focusing on a target (the center of the specification) and focusing on the tolerance (the allowable spread). A company that fails to focus on the target and allows the process to vary between tolerance limits faces loss. This loss exists because the product or service is varying from the desired target. For instance, if a cereal box is supposed to hold 12 ounces, if it holds more than 12 ounces, the company loses money. If it holds less than 12 ounces, the customer won't be happy because they are shorted cereal.

2.14 The traditional approach to quality emphasizes conformance to requirements, usually a specification with +/- limits. The Taguchi Loss Function points out that any deviation from the target specification results in a loss.

2.15 Dr. Deming's Red Bead experiment is a tool which describes the effects of processes and variation on worker performance. With the experiment, Deming is able to show that processes and systems can create situations where an employee can be performing to the best of their ability, yet still not be able to perform to a high standard, because the process is not providing appropriate input. The experiment also shows the effect of variation on a process.

2.16 Dr. Deming's Funnel experiment shows how randomly adjusting the process can lead to poorer quality. The focus should be on the target, the process should be allowed to settle down to its normal operating level, then the process can be examined for potential improvements that will enable it to achieve the target each time. Read Real Tools for Real Life example about tampering with the process.

2.17 Dr. Deming's system of profound knowledge has four parts:
An appreciation for a system
Knowledge about variation
Theory of knowledge
Psychology

An appreciation for how a system works is key to improvement. People working with the system must understand how the different parts of a system interact in order to produce a product or provide a service. Once this is understood, the entire system can be optimized and made more effective.
Knowledge of variation enables a problem solver to understand whether or not they are dealing with common cause or special cause variation. Improvements made to remove common cause variation from the system involve changing processes, changing the way work gets done. Special cause variation requires specific changes to prevent the special cause from happening again.

Theory of knowledge means that the person has an understanding of the how the process is performing. Knowledge comes from using performance measures to monitor the process and any process changes. Measures can reveal trends, patterns, and other anomalies. Psychology refers to the need to understand people and how they interact with each other.

2.18   a. Doctors: actual experience: doesn't want patient to get sick from other bacteria
           Stated/unstated: sterile equipment/clean environment/infection control
           Conscious/merely sensed: sterile equipment and good hygiene/ overall hospital
           cleanliness and employee compliance with hand washing requirements
           Technically operational/subjective: antibacterial soap/how long washing takes
        Nurses: actual experience: doesn't want patient to get sick from other bacteria
           Stated/unstated: sterile equipment/clean environment/infection control
           Conscious/merely sensed: sterile equipment and good hygiene/ overall hospital
           cleanliness and employee compliance with hand washing requirements
           Technically operational/subjective: antibacterial soap/how long washing takes
        Patients: actual experience: doesn't want to get sick from other bacteria
           Stated/unstated: sterile equipment/clean environment/infection control and staff that
           cares about infection risk
           Conscious/merely sensed: sterile equipment and good hygiene/ overall hospital
           cleanliness and employee compliance with hand washing requirements
           Technically operational/subjective: antibacterial soap/how long washing takes
        b. Several common causes would be: weakness of patients so they are susceptible to bacteria, existence of bacteria due to the very nature of hospital, number of visitors and patients in hospital who could transmit disease.
        c. Several assignable causes would be: no sinks in room, broken sinks in room, no towels or soap in room, no training in hand washing techniques.
         d. Institute leadership. Leadership must stress the importance of this problem by providing funding and support and holding people accountable for making improvements.
        e. Little q focuses on the small processes within a single area. Big Q focuses on the overall picture. Big Q takes a larger view of the situation and would institute a hospital wide improvement program to solve this problem.
        f. The economics of quality. Here the economics of quality can be clearly quantified as the costs of treating patients who contract other diseases or illnesses. Their deaths, loss of work time, suffering can all be quantified. These costs can be used to counterbalance and justify improvements.

Chapter 3

3.1   The purpose of a well-written problem statement is to serve as a guide for the problem-solving efforts. A problem statement helps team members stay focused on the task at hand.

3.2   See Figures 3.1 and 3.2

3.3   See Figures 3.1 and 3.2

3.4   Identify and implement methods to reduce the number of bike thefts on campus.

3.5   See Figures 3.1 and 3.2

3.6   A structured problem-solving process allows us to work systematically through an issue in search of the real reasons behind these issues. A structured problem-solving process keeps the focus on finding a true solution. A structured problem-solving process insists on checking the solution too. Follow the steps presented in Figure 3.1.

3.7   To create a problem statement, three guides to use are: to ensure it is phrased from the customer's point of view, to not list potential solutions in the problem statement, and to phrase it as clearly and concisely as possible.

3.8   The goal of good problem solving is to eliminate the root cause of the problem. In order to make sure the problem doesn't come back, Dr. Deming's Plan-Do-Study-Act cycle should be used to clarify the problem, map the process, analyze the situation, determine the root cause, create a plan to eliminate the root cause, implement a solution, determine if the solution is working, and ensure permanence of the solution.

3.9

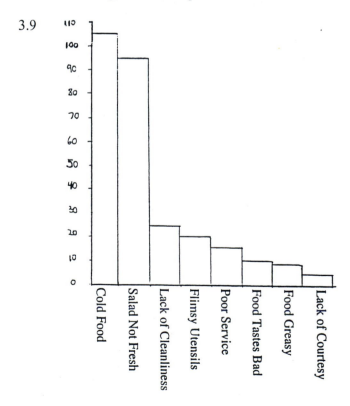

3.10

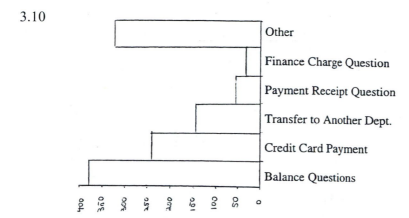

The "Other" column must be investigated and further pareto analysis must be done on breaking down what composed the "Other" column.

3.11 Once the Pareto chart has been created, the quality improvement team would focus on the most likely area in need of improvement. In this case, the size of the 'other' column is nearly as large as that of 'Balance Questions'. Steps to use this Pareto diagram would include further investigation into why 'other' has such a large amount of occurrences as well as an investigation into what can be done to reduce the number of customers who have questions concerning their balance.

3.12 Upon completing the charts, the upholsterers analyze them. Loose threads are involved in the greatest number of occurrences, followed by incorrect hemming. From a cost perspective, the greatest dollar loss is found in loose threads and pattern alignment errors. These will be the first areas they will investigate to seek the root causes associated with these occurrences.

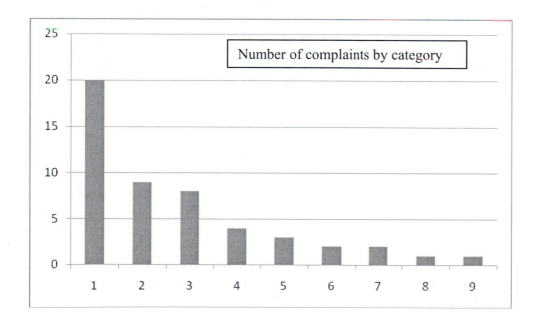

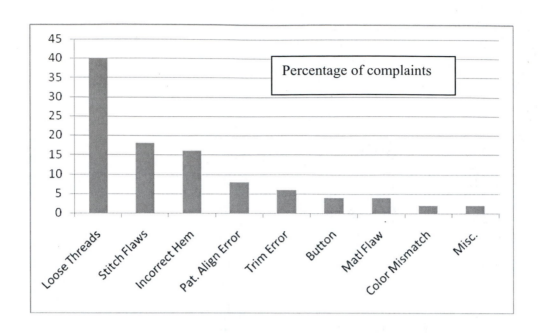

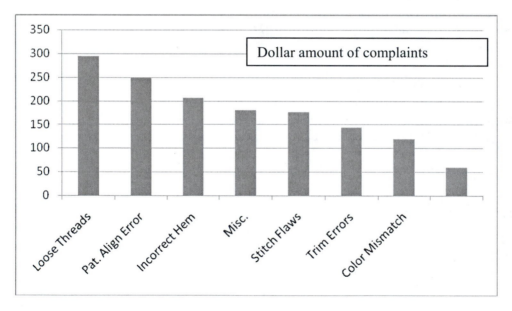

3.15   Based on the Pareto diagrams, PT Tool should be concentrating their improvement efforts on determining why the mounting plate is incorrectly mounted as well as why there are so many scratches on the surface of their landing gear.

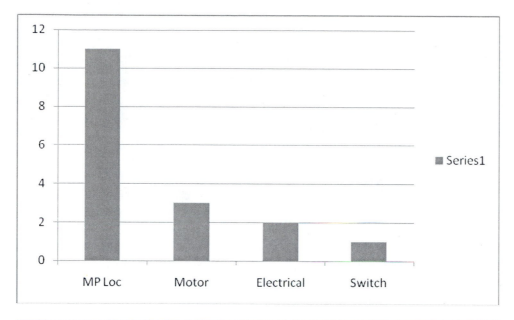

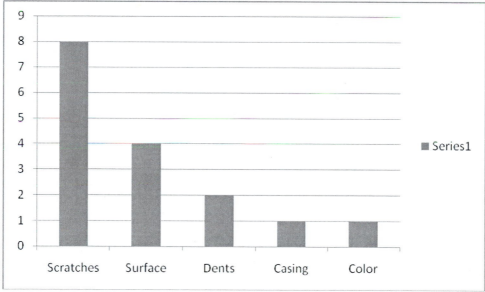

3.16   Based on the Pareto diagrams constructed using dollar amounts, PT Tool should be investigating Electrical system malfunctions (very costly) and damage to the casings. This is significantly different from the direction the investigation would take if only the count of non-conforming incidents was utilized to make a decision.

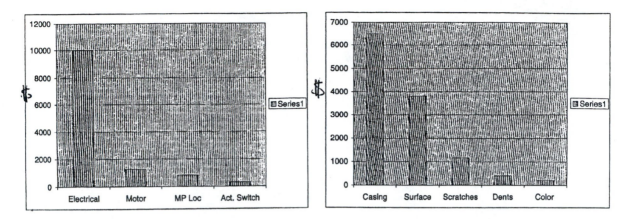

3.18   Number of calls completed per hour
Number of callers that receive a busy signal
Number of reoccurrences of line failure

3.19   Number of complaints in a particular category
Number of potential customers who leave before ordering
Number of compliments in a particular category
Number of repeat customers

3.20   Number of complaints in a particular category
Number of potential customers who leave before ordering
Number of compliments in a particular category
Number of repeat customers
Dollar loss per category

3.21   Number of occurrences in a particular category
Dollar loss per category to fix problems

3.22   Order taken wrong
Kitchen backed up
Waiter unaware order is ready
Waiter has too many tables
Order prepared wrong
Guest not a table
Large number of patrons in restaurant
Large party at table
Order overcooked/undercooked
Waiter dropped it

3.24

Merchandise	**Sales Person**	**Point of Sales System**	**Store Layout**
No sizes	Can't identify who is sales person	Types of charge cards taken	Cluttered
Limited selection	Sales person not around	Easy order entry	Difficult lines of vision
Not able to check another store	Too many customers for number of sales people	Completeness of receipt	Can't identify sales person
		Ease to make corrections	Lighting
		Ease to make markdowns	Location of registers
		Not able to ship	Not able to locate registers

3.25   Brainstorming gets all the ideas out so that they can be discussed. The dynamics of a brainstorming session allows people to build on each others ideas.

3.27

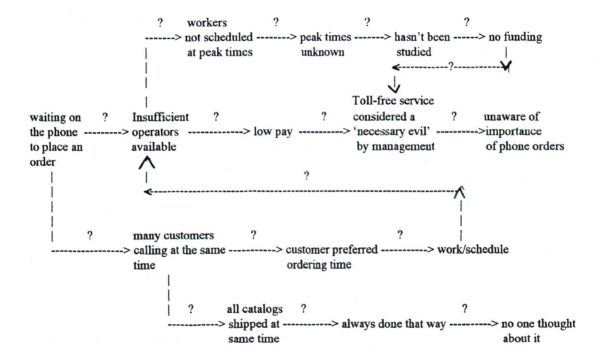

Actions:

Create measures and document importance of phone orders to bottom line. Present to management at monthly meetings.
Provide funding to study the timing of calls.
Utilize information about timing of calls and Queuing theory to schedule employees.
Study activities surrounding advertizing and promotions.

3.29

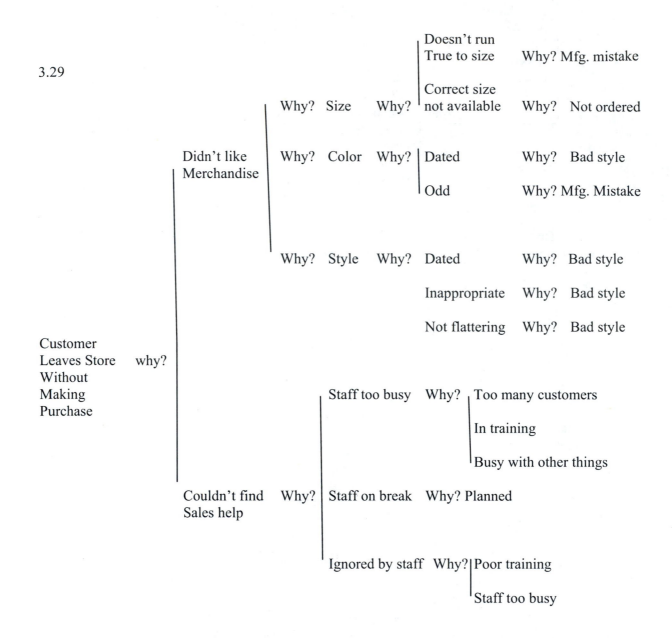

The store should reconsider its merchandizing (bad style) and they should plan breaks better and include training for the staff.

3.30   Process mapping an excellent problem solving tool because it helps everyone creating and using it understand how the company does the work it does. It reveals points of confusion, overlap, difficulty, and lack of clarity in a process.

3.31

Registration Flowchart

For freshman

Accepted at UD → Get registration material → Check the day to schedule → Make appointment with Advisor → Find out about classes/ Read material → Determine which classes interest you → Determine prerequisits for classes → Prioritize classes

for upperclassman

Decide if coming back → Get registration material

Prioritize classes → Talk with friends about classes → Choose what classes to take

Choose what classes to take — No → (back)
Choose what classes to take — Yes → Look at schedule → Discover which Prof. teaches classes → Check class overlay

Check class overlay — Yes → (back)
Check class overlay — No → Check for schedule conflicts

Check for schedule conflicts — Yes → Check class closed list
Check for schedule conflicts — No → (back)

Check class closed list — No → Go to bursar → Pay outstanding Bursar bill → Go to advisor's appointment → Converse with Advisor about classes
Check class closed list — Yes → (up)

Converse with Advisor about classes → Advisor approves schedule

Advisor approves schedule — No → (back)
Advisor approves schedule — Yes → Fill out forms → Advisor signs forms → You sign forms → Over 17Hrs Go to Dean

Over 17Hrs Go to Dean — Yes → Make appointment with Dean → Meet with Dean and explain situation → Dean Signature → Check closed class list
Over 17Hrs Go to Dean — No → Check closed class list

Check closed class list — Yes → Get closed list permission from academic Chairman
Check closed class list — No → Stand in line WAIT (Almost there!)

Get closed list permission from academic Chairman — No → (back)
Get closed list permission from academic Chairman — Yes → Stand in line WAIT (Almost there!)

Stand in line WAIT (Almost there!) → REGISTER!!!

13

3.33

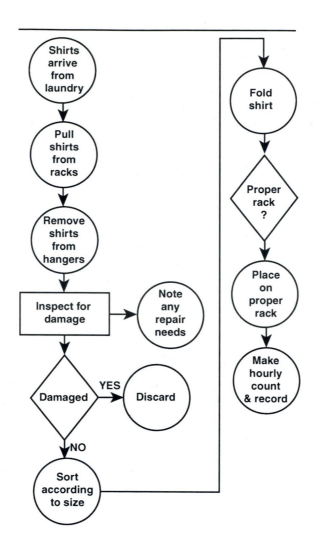

3.36   A cause and effect diagram is a great problem solving tool because it organizes brainstorming sessions and ideas. It shows where patterns exist. Its organization allows for clearer discussion of the problem. It keeps people focused.

3.37   Cause and effect diagrams play a role in finding the root cause of a problem because they allow for clearer, more organized discussion of problems. Cause and effect diagrams keep people focused on the topic at hand.

3.38

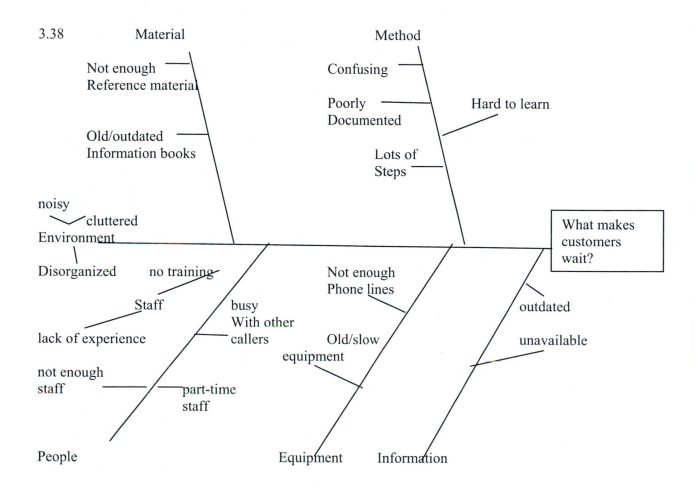

3.40

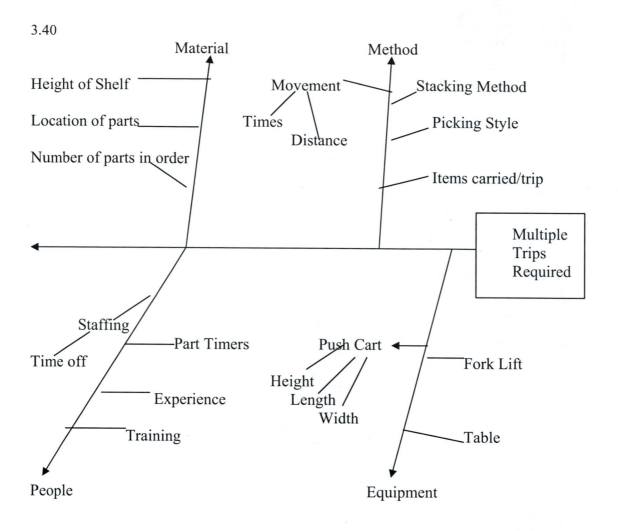

3.41

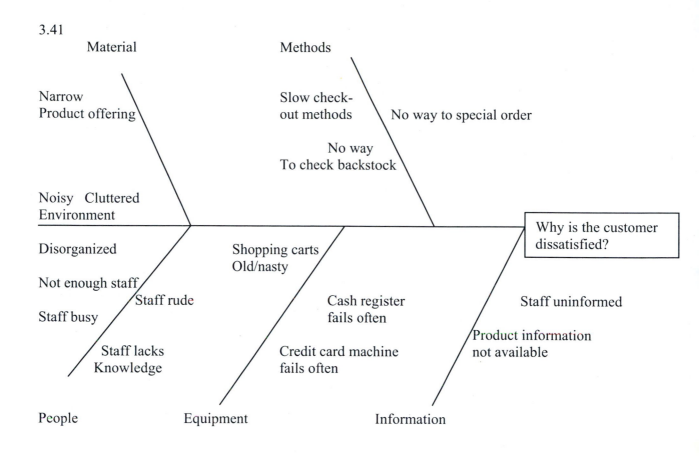

3.42

Reduce Order Picking Time

Driving Force	Restraining Force
Sales increase	Expense
Stress decreases	Old method ingrained
Productivity	Reorganization of warehouse
Increases	time consuming
	Loss of revenue during change

1. Reorganize a section of the warehouse at a time
2. Begin reorganization during Christmas shutdown
3. Have changes stages for ease of implementation

Force Field Analysis
Bikes being stolen on campus

Driving Forces	Restraining Forces
1. Students are upset about bike thefts	1. Administration unconcerned about problem
2. Loss of bike costly	2. Funding required to update existing bike parking areas
3. Poor image for school	3. Funding required to create new bike parking areas
4. Hassle for student	4. Limited space available for bike parking areas
5. Requires campus police intervention which is costly	

Plan of Action

1. Create awareness in administration concerning severity of problem. Give them the facts.
2. Provide designated parking facilities for bikes, including bike racks.
3. Place designated parking facilities for bikes in conspicuous location.

WAIT FOR FOOD EXCEEDS 10 MINUTES

WAIT FOR FOOD EXCEEDS 10 MINUTES

IMPROVED COMMUNICATION AND STANDARDIZATION

Driving Forces

Increase customer satisfaction

Increase employee satisfaction

Reduce time wait for food

Increase business turnover

Improve the atmosphere

Reduce congestion and mistaken orders

Reduce menu mixups

Reduce carryout and eat-in order mixups

Improve employee performance

Restraining Forces

Money for new menus

Time for retraining and standardizing method

Attitude of workers

New equipment availability

Space for new equipment

Plan of Action

1. Standardize menus.

2. Standardize order-taking process, order placing process, cooking methods, and check-out and check-in process.

3. Separate luncheons of eat-in and carryout.

4. Instruct employees on new items, unavailability of food, and specials.

5. Stress the idea and include education on quality and continuous improvement.

3.48

a. Describe the steps found in Figure 3.1 and Table 3.1

b. The 80-20 rule refers to the 'vital few'. Pareto diagrams are created in order to determine which problems are the worst and therefore should be worked on first. In this case, incorrect, late, incomplete paperwork is the problem that occurs the most frequently. Solving it will provide the greatest improvement to the process.

c. # of surgeries cancelled
   # of surgeries rescheduled
   # of surgeries cancelled within one hour of planned surgery
   # of patient complaints
   # of time doctors/anesthesiologists/nurses are paid for surgeries that were cancelled.

d.

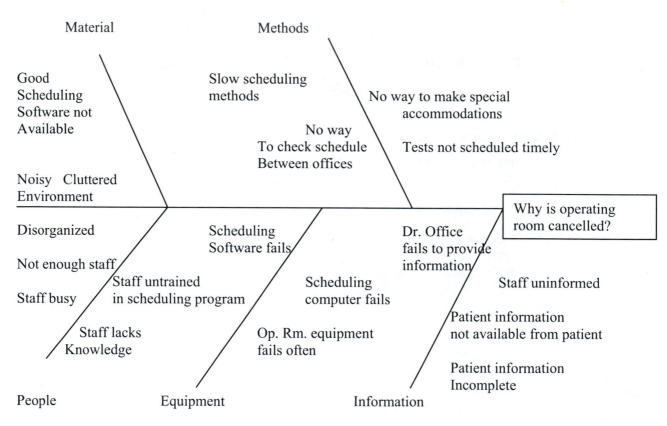

e.

```
                                                                    Too busy          Why? Sch. mistake

                                    Why?  Doctor  Why?  not available     Why?   Poor Comm
                                          N.A.

                Couldn't             Why?  Patient  Why? │ Doesn't know   Why?   Poor
                Match                       N.A.          │ Dates/times          Communication
                Schedules
                                                          │ Unaware Why?PoorCommunication


                                    Why?  Test     Why?  Dated          Why?   Old Installation
                                          Facility
                                          N.A.            Inappropriate  Why?   Equipment
                                                          Facility               N.A.

                                                          Equipment      Why? Poor Planning
Correct                                                   N.A.
Tests        why?
Not
Performed                                 Staff too busy  Why? ┌ Too many customers

                                                              │ In training

                                                              └ Busy with other things

                Couldn't             Why? │ Staff on break  Why? Planned
                Schedule
                Test

                                          │ Ignored by staff  Why?│ Poor training

                                                                  └ Staff too busy
```

21

f.

The number of Hospital surgeries cancelled is too high

Driving Forces

Increase customer satisfaction

Increase employee satisfaction

Reduce time wait for surgery rooms

Increase business turnover.

Improve the atmosphere.

Reduce congestion

Reduce # of surgery rescheduled

Reduce waste of time/effort/material

Improve employee performance

Restraining Forces

Old methodologies in place

No communication between departments

Lack of cooperation between departments

Large number of doctors to deal with

Plan of Action

1. Standardize method for communicating with doctors' offices.

2. Standardize surgical room scheduling process and check-out and check-in process.

3. Improve communication between scheduler and doctors' offices by utilizing new computer methods.

4. Instruct employees on new methods and computer.

5. Include education on quality and continuous improvement.

Chapter 4

4.1   Sample: A small portion of a population that, when analyzed, may provide information concerning the entire population.

Population: The total set of observations being considered in a statistical procedure.

4.2   Continuous statistic:
           -weight of 5 pound bag of flour
           -millimeters separating a closed car door from its frame
           -amount of cutting fluid used during a particular machining operation

Discrete statistic:
           -number of 5 pound bags of flour produced
           -number of cars passing through a toll booth
           -number of telephone calls received in one hour

4.5

```
                                        X
                              X    X    X
                         X    X    X    X    X
         X    X    X    X    X    X    X    X    X    X
       _____
        220  221  222  223  224  225  226  227  228  229  230
```

Skewed to the left.

4.6   Range = 12 − 1 = 11

$$i = \frac{11}{3} + 1 = 5 \quad \leftarrow \text{choose}$$

$$i = \frac{11}{5} + 1 = 3$$

First Cell Midpoint = 1
Other Midpoints = 4, 7, 10

Boundaries = 0, 2.5, 5.5, 8.5, 11.5, 14.5

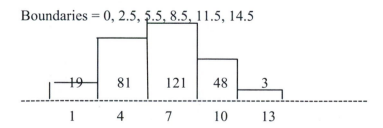

This histogram is uni-modal, skewed slightly to the right, some variance, and resembles a normal curve.

4.7

0.6535	x
0.6540	xxxxx xxxxx xxx
0.6545	xxxxx
0.6550	x
0.6555	
0.6560	
0.6565	
0.6570	x
0.6575	xx
0.6580	xxxxx xxxx
0.6585	xxx
0.6590	xx
0.6595	xxx

4.8

4	/
5	/
6	///
7	/////
8	///// //
9	////
10	///
11	//
12	/
13	/

4.9

0.001	
0.002	//
0.003	/
0.004	///
0.005	
0.006	//
0.007	/
0.008	
0.009	/
0.010	///
0.011	////
0.012	///
0.013	/
0.014	/
0.015	///
0.016	
0.017	/
0.018	//
0.019	
0.020	////
0.021	

4.10 $R = X_h - X_l = 0.020 - 0.002 = 0.018$

$$h = \frac{R}{i} + 1 = \frac{0.018}{i} + 1$$

When i = 0.003, h = 7
When i = 0.005, h = 5 ←Choose
When i = 0.007, h = 4

Midpoints
    0.002, 0.007, 0.012, 0.017, 0.022

Boundaries of cells
    0.002 +/−0.0025

    0, 0.0045
    0.0045, 0.0095
    0.0095, 0.0145
    0.0145, 0.0195,
    0.0195, 0.0245

4.11 $R = 13 - 4 = 9$

$$h = \frac{9}{3} + 1 = 4$$

Lowest Midpoint = 4
Other Midpoints = 7, 10, 13

Boundaries = 2.5, 5.5, 8.5, 11.5, 14.5

This histogram is uni-modal, skewed slightly to the right, low variance, and resembles a normal curve.

4.12 $R = X_h - X_l = 150 - 125 \quad 25$

$$h = \frac{R}{i} + 1 = \frac{25}{i} + 1$$

When $i = 3, h = 9$
         $i = 5, h = 6 \leftarrow$ choose
         $i = 7, h = 5$

Lowest midpoint = 125

Boundaries of first cell
    125 +/−2.5

4.13 $R = X_h - X_l = 10 - 1 = 9$

$$h = \frac{R}{i} + 1 = \frac{9}{i} + 1$$

When $i = 3, h = 4 \leftarrow$ choose
         $i = 5, h = 2.8$
         $i = 7, h = 2.3$

Lowest Midpoint = 1

Boundaries of first cell
    1 +/−1.5

4.14 $R = Xh - Xl = 120.2 - 119.4 = 0.8$

$$h = \frac{R}{i} + 1 = \frac{0.8}{i} + 1$$

When $i = 0.3$, $h = 3.7$ ←choose
   $i = 0.5$, $h = 2.6$
   $i = 0.7$, $h = 2.1$

Lowest Midpoint

119.4

This histogram is nearly symmetrical,
Slightly skewed to the right. It is
uni-modal.

Boundaries of first cell
   119.4 +/–0.15
   or 119.25 to 119.55

4.15 The distribution is not symmetrical, it is skewed to the left (negatively skewed).

4.16 It is important to use both statistical measures and descriptive concepts when describing a histogram. The statistical measures describe the distribution mathematically while the descriptive concepts provide a visual picture of the distribution. Combining both creates a greater understanding of the process.

4.17 Range = 0.006
   $MP_L = 0.6535$

try $i = 0.0003$; $h = \dfrac{0.006}{0.0003} + 1 = 21$

try $i = 0.0005$; $h = \dfrac{0.006}{0.0005} + 1 = 13$

try $i = 0.0007$; $h = \dfrac{0.006}{0.0007} + 1 = 10$

try $i = 0.0009$; $h = \dfrac{0.006}{0.0009} + 1 = 8$ ←use

1st cell boundary $= 0.6535 - \dfrac{i}{2} = 0.6535 - \dfrac{0.0009}{2} = 0.65305$

Cell Boundaries	Cell Midpoints	Frequency
0.65305 – 0.65395	0.6535	I
0.65395 – 0.65485	0.6544	IIIII IIIII IIIII III
0.65485 – 0.65575	0.6559	I
0.65575 – 0.65665	0.6562	
0.65665 – 0.65755	0.6571	III
0.65755 – 0.65845	0.658	IIIII III
0.65845 – 0.65935	0.6589	IIIII III
0.65935 – 0.66055	0.6598	III

4.18   R = 38 − 14 = 24

$$i = \frac{24}{3} + 1 = 9$$

$$i = \frac{24}{5} + 1 = 6 \leftarrow \text{choose}$$

$$i = \frac{24}{7} + 1 = 5$$

$$i = \frac{24}{9} + 1 = 4$$

Lowest Midpoint = 14
Other Midpoints = 19, 24, 28, 33

Boundaries = 10.5, 15.5, 20.5, 25.5, 30.5, 35.5

This histogram is uni-modal, skewed slightly to the right, high variance, and resembles a normal curve.

4.19   The central tendency of the data refers to describing where the data is grouped in relation to the desired target value. The central tendency is described by the mean, the mode and the median.

4.20   Measures of dispersion refer to the spread of the data in the distribution or around the desired target. Measures of dispersion are the range and the standard deviation.

4.21   The salary data for the engineer includes key information concerning the standard deviation and the range (min, max). The size of the sample (n) is also significantly larger, providing more information. This additional information gives validity to the average of $48,298 and median of $45,750.

4.22   Mean = 8   Mode = 8, Median = 8

4.23   Mean = 1.123
        Mode = 1.122
        Median = 1.123

4.24   Mean = 0.656
        Mode = 0.654
        Median = 0.655

28

4.25   Mean = 226.2
Mode = 227
Median = 227
$\sigma = 2.36$

4.26   Mean = 0.011
Mode = 0.011, 0.020
Median = 0.011
Standard Deviation = 0.009
Range = 0.02

These values confirm that the histogram spreads widely. While the mean and median are nearly equal, two modes exist.

4.27   Mean = 141
Mode = 146
Median = 142
Standard Deviation = 6
Range = 25

These values confirm that the histogram has a broad spread. The mean, mode and median are nearly equal, a slight skew to the left exists.

4.28   Mean = 119.8
Mode = 119.8
Median = 119.8
Standard Deviation = 0.2
Range = 0.8
        These values confirm that the histogram has a narrow spread. The mean, mode and median are equal. The distribution is symmetrical.

4.29 $\sigma = 5.32$
R = 9

4.30 $\sigma = 0.0022$
R = 0.0065

4.31   Mean = 0.656
Mode = 0.654
Median = 0.655
$\sigma = 0.0022$

4.32   Mean = 0.077
$\sigma = 0.0032$

4.33   Mean = 24
Mode = 25
Median = 25
Range = 19
$\sigma = 5$

4.34   The mean, mode, median, standard deviation, and the range work together to describe a histogram by providing analytical information concerning where the data is located, i.e., the central tendency of the data and the dispersion of the data. This information allows those investigating a process to understand the process's accuracy and precision.

4.35   The distribution is slightly negatively skewed. The mean is less than the median which is less than the mode. Without mathematical data, the range and standard deviation can not be easily judged, though the distribution does lack a long tail indicative of a large standard deviation or range. The kurtosis can not be judged because there are no other curves to compare it with.

4.36   The middle curve has a significantly larger standard deviation than the acceptable curve for the process. It is platykurtic. The curve on the right has a significantly smaller standard deviation than the acceptable curve for the process. It is leptokurtic.

4.37

$$Z = \frac{15 - 8}{3} = 2.33$$

Area = 0.9893 Percentage of calls lasting over 15 minutes => 1 – 0.9893 = 0.0107
1.1% of calls last over 15 minutes

4.38 $$Z = \frac{15 - 12}{3} = 1$$
Area = 0.8413
            84.13% wait less than 15 minutes

4.39 $$Z = \frac{(0.25 - 0.917)}{0.005} = 1.60$$
Area = 0.9452
1 – 0.9452 = 0.0548
            5.48% above 90 mm

4.40 $$Z = \frac{65 - 70}{3} = \frac{-5}{3} = -1.67$$
Area = 0.0475
Area = 1 – 0.0475 = 0.9525
            95.25% acceptable

4.42   X-bar = 20.6

std dev = 1.3 $$Z = \frac{19.7 - 20.6}{1.3} = -0.69$$

Xi = 19.7

The amount of product produced that falls below the lower specification limit of 19.7 pounds is 24.51%.

4.43   X-bar = 44.795

std dev = 0.402 $Z = \dfrac{44.000 - 44.795}{0.402} = -1.98$

Xi = 44.000

The percentage of coils produced that falls below the minimum requirement of 44.000 is 2.4%.

4.44   X-bar = 50

std dev = 18 $Z = \dfrac{0 - 50}{18} = -2.78$

Xi = 0

Area = 0.0027

X-bar = 50

std dev = 18 $Z = \dfrac{90 - 50}{18} = -2.22$

Xi = 90

Area = 0.9868

The percentage of temperatures that falls between 0 and 90 degrees is equal to 0.9868 − 0.0027 = 0.9841 or 98.41%.

4.45   X-bar = 119.8

std dev = 0.2 $Z = \dfrac{119.7 - 119.8}{0.2} = -0.5$

Xi = 119.7

X-bar = 119.8

std dev = 0.2 $Z = \dfrac{120.3 - 119.8}{0.2} = 2.5$

Xi = 120.3

The amount of product produced that falls below the lower specification limit of 119.7 mm is 30.85%
The amount of product produced that falls above the upper specification limit of 120.3 pounds is 1 − 0.9938 = 0.0062 or 0.62%.

These results verify that the process is not centered correctly in order to meet the specifications. The standard deviation is also large when compared to the narrow spread of the process.

4.46 $Z = \dfrac{65 - 45}{10} = 2.0$ $Area_1 = 0.9772$

         $Z = \dfrac{35 - 45}{10} = -1.0$ $Area_2 = 0.1587$

         $Area_3 = 0.9773 - 0.1587 = 0.8186$

                 81.86% of clean-ups take between 35 and 65 minutes.

4.47 $Z = \dfrac{X_i - 3000}{50} = -2.575$

         $-2.575 = \dfrac{X_i - 3000}{50}$

         $Xi = 2871.25$ foot-candles

4.48 $Z = \dfrac{1000 - 900}{50} = 2$

         $Area_1 = 0.9773$

         $Area_2 = 1 - 0.9773 = 0.0227$

                 2.27% of batteries survive beyond 1000 days

4.50 $Z = \dfrac{11.41 - 11.85}{1.33} = -0.33$

         $Area = 0.3707$

                 37.07% of parts will be below the lower specification limit of 11.41 inches.

4.51 $Z = \dfrac{25 - 23}{4} = 0.5$

         $Area = 0.6915$ $1 - 0.6915 = 0.3085$ 30.85% have hysteresis greater than 25.

4.52   Since $\alpha = 0.10$, then $Z(\alpha/2) = 1.645$

         $0.0015 +/- \dfrac{1.645(0.0008)}{\sqrt{32}} = (0.0017, 0.0013)$

         The engineers know with 90% confidence that the interval values for the population mean are (0.0017, 0.0013).

4.53   Since $\alpha = 0.05$, then $Z(\alpha/2) = 1.96$

         $1200 +/- \dfrac{1.96(100)}{\sqrt{40}} = (1231, 1169)$

         The manufacturer knows with 95% confidence that the interval values for the population mean are (1231, 1169).

4.54   Since $\alpha = 0.05$, then $t(\alpha/2) = 2.365$

         $44.795 +/- \dfrac{2.365(0.402)}{\sqrt{8}} = (45.131, 44.458)$

         At a 95% confidence level, the interval for the population mean is (45.131, 44.458).

4.55   Since $\alpha = 0.01$, then $Z(\alpha/2) = 2.575$

$$351 \pm \frac{2.575(2)}{\sqrt{50}} = (350, 352)$$

The chef knows with 99% confidence that the interval values for the population mean are (350, 352).

Chapter 5

5.1   Assignable or special causes occur when there is a specific, external reason for a change in the process. Assignable causes are the uncontrolled variation present in the process. This variation can be isolated as the cause of a change in the behavior of the process. Chance or common refer to causes that are internal to the process, they are present throughout the process. They are naturally occurring. This type of variation can be removed from the process only by changing the process itself.

5.2   To manage a group of people it is critical to determine whether or not they are being affected by either chance or assignable causes. This means that you must determine whether or not the cause effects the entire group (chance) or if it effects a single member of that group (assignable).

5.3 $n = 5$

$\overline{\overline{X}} = 16$ min $\overline{R} = 7$

$UCLx = 16 + (0.577)(7) = 20$ $UCLr = 2.115(7) = 15$
$LCLx = 16 - (0.577)(7) = 12$ $LCLr = 0(7) = 0$

5.4 $n = 4$

$\overline{\overline{X}} = 50.2$ $\overline{R} = 0.68$

$UCLx = 50.2 + (0.729)(0.68) = 50.7$ $UCLr = 2.282(0.68) = 1.6$
$LCLx = 50.2 - (0.729)(0.68) = 49.7$ $LCLr = 0(0.68) = 0$

Revising the chart:
Remove 5 points from both charts.

$$\overline{\overline{X}}new = \frac{1255 - 251.7}{25 - 5} = 50.2$$

$\overline{R}new = 0.67$

$$sigma = \frac{0.67}{2.059} = 0.325$$

$UCLx = 50.6$ $UCLr = 1.5$
$LCLx = 49.8$ $LCLr = 0$

5.5 $n = 5$ $\overline{\overline{X}} = \dfrac{4189}{12} = 349$ $\overline{R} = \dfrac{164}{12} = 14$

$UCL_X = 349 + (0.577)(14) = 357$
$LCL_X = 349 - (0.577)(14) = 341$

$UCL_R = 2.114(14) = 30$
$LCL_R = 0(4) = 0$

5.6 When a process is in a state of statistical control it exhibits no unusual patterns, trends or runs. Two-thirds of the points will be on or near the centerline, with no points beyond the control limits. The points will float freely back and forth across the centerline and they will be balanced on both sides of the centerline.

5.7 An X, and R or s chart under normal statistical control exhibits the following characteristics. Both charts will have no patterns, trends, or runs. There will be a few points on or near centerline. No points will be beyond the control limits. Two-thirds of the points will be near the centerline. The points will be balanced on both sides of the centerline and the points move freely back and forth across the centerline.

5.8 Accuracy is recognizable on the X chart by noting how the averages of the sample data are clustered around the centerline. Precision is recognizable on the R chart by noting the magnitude of the average R values.

5.9 The use and interpretation of an R or s chart is critical when examining an X chart because the R or s charts allow the user to see the spread of the data. The charts show if the spread of the data is reasonable for the measurements on the X chart. The R or s chart shows the repeatability of the process.

5.10 $n = 5$ $\bar{\bar{X}} = \dfrac{1.8798}{30} = 0.0627$ $\bar{R} = \dfrac{0.0102}{30} = 0.0003$

$UCL_x = 0.0627 + (0.577)(0.0003) = 0.0629$
$LCL_x = 0.0627 - (0.577)(0.0003) = 0.0625$

$UCL_R = 2.114(0.0003) = 0.0006$
$LCL_R = 0(0.0003) = 0$

5.11 $n = 8$
$\bar{\bar{X}} = 3.02$ $\bar{R} = 0.10$

$UCL_x = 3.02 + (0.373)(0.10) = 3.06$ $UCL_r = 1.864(0.10) = 0.19$
$LCL_x = 3.02 - (0.373)(0.10) = 2.98$ $LCL_r = 0.136(0.10) = 0.01$

5.12 On the X-bar chart, two-thirds of the points are not near the centerline. Three points are on or near the centerline. The points flow back and forth across the centerline. The points are balanced. There are no points beyond the control limits. There are no patterns or trends. There does appear to be a spiky appearance to the chart. There is a lot of variation present between subgroups. On the R chart, there is a lot of variation present in the process within the individual subgroups. The chart has a spiky appearance even though there are no points beyond the control limits. The points float back and forth across the centerline. The points are balanced. And there are several points near the centerline.

5.13 Both the X-bar and R chart show excellent control. On the X-bar chart, two-thirds of the points are near the centerline. Three points are on the centerline. The points flow back and forth across the centerline. The points are balanced. There are no points beyond the control limits. There are no patterns or trends. On the R chart, two-thirds of the points are near the centerline. The points are balanced. There are no points beyond the control limits. The points float back and forth across the centerline. The points are balanced. And there are several points near the centerline.

5.14 $\overline{\overline{X}} = \dfrac{0.0644}{23} = 0.0028$ $\qquad$ $\overline{R} = \dfrac{0.0133}{23} = 0.0006$

$UCL_X = 0.0028 + (0.729)(0.0006) = 0.0032$
$LCL_X = 0.0028 - (0.729)(0.0006) = 0.0024$

$UCL_R = 2.282(0.0006) = 0.0014$
$LCL_R = 0(0.0006) = 0$

5.15 $\overline{\overline{X}} = \dfrac{646}{18} = 36$ $\qquad$ $\overline{R} = \dfrac{36}{18} = 2$

$UCL_X = 36 + (1.023)(2) = 38$
$LCL_X = 36 - (1.023)(2) = 34$

$UCL_R = 2.574(2) = 5$
$LCL_R = 0$

5.16 $\overline{\overline{X}} = \dfrac{1500.2}{20} = 75$ $\qquad$ $\overline{R} = \dfrac{35.2}{20} = 1.8$

$UCL_X = 75 + (0.577)(1.8) = 76$
$LCL_X = 75 - (0.577)(1.8) = 74$

$UCL_R = 2.114(1.8) = 3.8$
$LCL_R = 0$

5.17 $\overline{\overline{X}} = \dfrac{30.48}{20} = 1.52$ $\qquad$ $\overline{R} = \dfrac{1.36}{20} = 0.07$

$UCL_X = 1.52 + (0.729)(0.07) = 1.57$
$LCL_X = 1.52 - (0.729)(0.07) = 1.47$

$UCL_R = 2.282(0.07) = 0.16$
$LCL_R = 0$

5.18 $\overline{\overline{X}} = \dfrac{528}{20} = 26.4$ $\overline{R} = \dfrac{51.9}{20} = 2.6$

$UCL_X = 26.4 + (1.427)(2.6) = 30.1$
$LCL_X = 26.4 - (1.427)(2.6) = 22.7$

$UCL_R = 2.089(2.6) = 5.4$
$LCL_R = 0$

5.19 $\overline{\overline{X}} = \dfrac{1.8798}{30} = 0.0627$ $\overline{S} = \dfrac{0.0042}{30} = 0.0001$

$UCL_X = 0.0627 + (1.427)(0.0001) = 0.0628$
$LCL_X = 0.0627 - (1.427)(0.0001) = 0.0626$

$UCL_S = 2.089(0.0001) = 0.0002$
$LCL_S = 0(0.0001) = 0$

5.20 $\overline{\overline{X}} = \dfrac{0.0643}{23} = 0.0028$ $\overline{S} = \dfrac{0.0061}{23} = 0.0003$

$UCL_X = 0.0028 + (1.628)(0.0003) = 0.0033$
$LCL_X = 0.0028 - (1.628)(0.0003) = 0.0023$

$UCL_S = 2.266(0.0003) = 0.0007$
$LCL_S = 0(0.0003) = 0$

5.21   The Sigma chart exhibits no patterns, runs or trends. The points float back and forth across the centerline, they are balanced, and many of the points are near or on the centerline. The X-bar chart is also in a state of control.

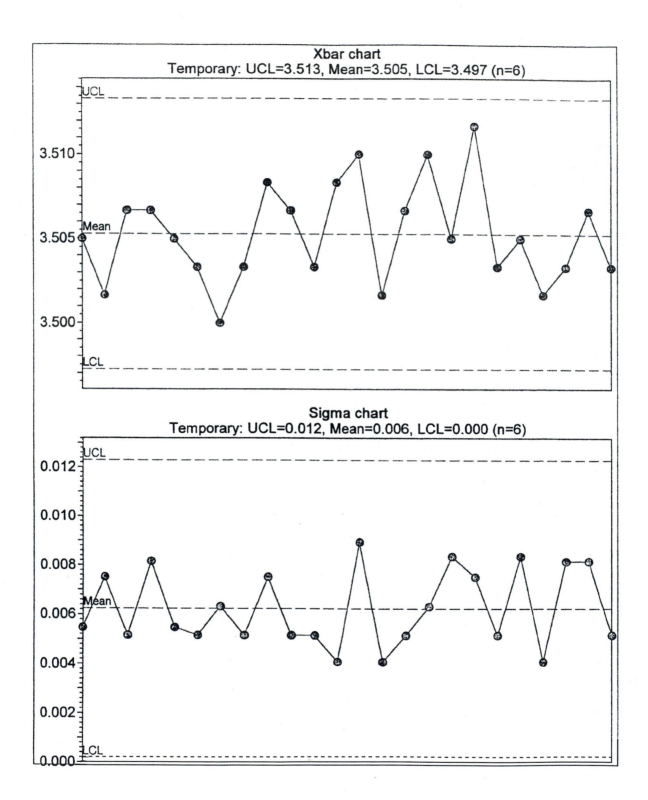

5.23   The Sigma chart exhibits no patterns, runs, or trends. The points float back and forth across the centerline, they are balanced, and many of the points are near or on the centerline. The X-bar chart exhibits a definite cycle. By studying the chart, it is obvious that the South location in the plant has consistently high air particulate readings. The East location in the plant has consistently low air particulate readings.

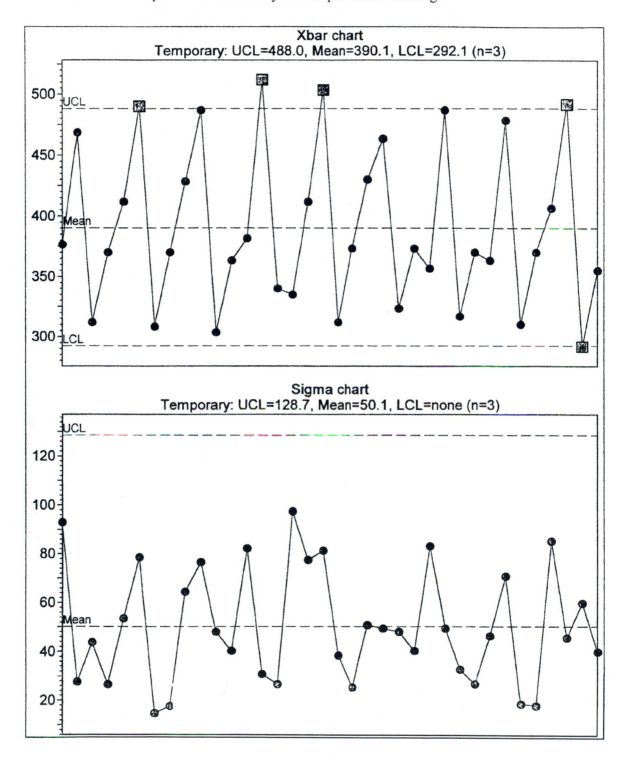

5.24 $\overline{\overline{X}} = \dfrac{600.823}{10} = 60.082$ $\text{s-bar} = \dfrac{0.043}{10} = 0.004$

$UCL_X = 60.082 + (1.954)(0.004) = 60.090$
$LCL_X = 60.082 - (1.954)(0.004) = 60.074$

$UCL_s = 2.568(0.004) = 0.010$
$LCL_s = 0$

Chapter 6

6.1   Control limits represent the boundaries of the process. They help predict future process behavior. Specification limits are set by the designer. They represent the expectations of the designer or customer. If the process is capable (Case 1), the 6σ will be less than the spread of the specification limits. In case 2, the spread of the specifications and the 6σ spread of the process are equal. There is no room for error. In case 3, 6σ spread more widely than the specification limits, the process is not capable.

6.2   Specifications describe the expectations of the customer. Control limits describe the performance of the process. To determine whether or not a process is capable of meeting the expectations of the customer, USL – LSL must be greater than 6σ.

6.3   A capable process is a process that is producing to the best of its ability (consistently, precisely, accurately) and exhibiting control (6 checks from Chapter 5). A process can be in control but not capable of meeting specifications when the specifications set by the designer/customer are narrower in spread than the spread of the process as shown by 6 sigma. The realities of the process can not be forced to meet the desires of the customer. The process must be improved.

6.4
$$\sigma = \frac{\overline{R}}{d_2} = \frac{7}{2.326} = 3$$

$$6\sigma = 18$$

$$C_p = \frac{U - L}{6\sigma} = \frac{21 - 13}{18} = 0.44$$

$$C_{pk} = \frac{Z(min)}{3}$$

$$Z(U) = \frac{(U - \overline{X})}{\sigma} = \frac{21 - 16}{3} = 1.66$$

$$Z(L) = \frac{(\overline{X} - L)}{\sigma} = \frac{16 - 13}{3} = 1$$

$$C_{pk} = \frac{1}{3} = 0.33$$

Process is not capable and not centered.

6.5   Emphasizing the target specification encourages a focus on narrowing the spread of the process by reducing variation. When working to the specification limits, there is limited emphasis on reducing variation because any performance between the specification limits· is acceptable.

6.6 $\quad \sigma = \dfrac{\overline{R}}{d_2} = \dfrac{0.68}{2.059} = 0.33$

$6\sigma = 1.98$

$Cp = \dfrac{U - L}{6\sigma} = \dfrac{50.5 - 49.5}{1.98} = 0.51$

$Cpk = \dfrac{Z(min)}{3} \qquad\qquad$ X-bar = 50.2, n = 4

$Z(U) = \dfrac{U - \overline{X}}{\sigma} = \dfrac{50.5 - 50.2}{0.33} = 0.91$

$Z(L) = \dfrac{\overline{X} - L}{\sigma} = \dfrac{50.2 - 49.5}{0.33} = 2.12$

$Cpk = \dfrac{0.91}{3} = 0.3$

The process is not capable of meeting specifications and not centered.

6.7 $\quad \sigma = \dfrac{\overline{R}}{d_2} = \dfrac{0.00014}{2.326} = 0.00006$

$6\sigma = 0.00036$

$Cp = \dfrac{U - L}{6\sigma} = \dfrac{0.50370 - 0.50330}{0.00036} = 1.1$

$Cpk = \dfrac{Z(min)}{3} \qquad\qquad$ X-bar = 0.50349, n = 5

$Z(U) = \dfrac{U - \overline{X}}{\sigma} = \dfrac{0.50370 - 0.50349}{0.00006} = 3.5$

$Z(L) = \dfrac{\overline{X} - L}{\sigma} = \dfrac{0.50349 - 0.50330}{0.00006} = 3.17$

$Cpk = \dfrac{3.17}{3} = 1.1$

The process is capable of meeting specifications and centered.

6.8 $\quad \sigma = \dfrac{\text{s-bar}}{c_4} = \dfrac{1}{0.693} = 1$

$Cp = \dfrac{36 - 30}{6(1)} = 1.0$

$Cpk = \dfrac{2}{3} = 0.66$

Where:

$Z(u) = \dfrac{36 - 32}{1} = 4$

$Z(l) = \dfrac{32 - 30}{1} = 2$

The process is not centered and just barely capable.

6.9 $Cp = \dfrac{10-8}{6(1.446)} = 0.23$

$Cpk = \dfrac{0.43}{3} = 0.14$

Where:

$Z(u) = \dfrac{10-8.624}{1.446} = 0.95$

$Z(l) = \dfrac{8.624-8}{1.446} = 0.43$

The process is not capable and not centered.

6.10 $\sigma = \dfrac{\text{R-bar}}{d_2} = \dfrac{2}{2.059} = 1$

$Cp = \dfrac{29-23}{6(1)} = 1$

$Cpk = \dfrac{2}{3} = 0.66$

Where:

$Z(u) = \dfrac{29-25}{1} = 4$

$Z(l) = \dfrac{25-23}{1} = 2$

The process is capable but not centered.

6.11 $\sigma = \dfrac{\overline{R}}{d_2} = \dfrac{0.10}{2.847} = 0.04$

$6\sigma = 0.24$

$Cp = \dfrac{U-L}{6\sigma} = \dfrac{3.05-2.95}{0.24} = 0.42$

$Cpk = \dfrac{Z(min)}{3}$ X-bar = 3.02, n = 8

$Z(U) = \dfrac{U-\overline{X}}{\sigma} = \dfrac{3.05-3.02}{0.04} = 0.8$

$Z(L) = \dfrac{(\overline{X}-L)}{\sigma} = \dfrac{3.02-2.95}{0.04} = 1.8$

$Cpk = \dfrac{0.8}{3} = 0.27$

The process is not capable of meeting specifications and not centered.

6.12 $\quad \sigma = \dfrac{\overline{R}}{d_2} = \dfrac{0.0006}{2.059} = 0.0003$

$6\sigma = 0.0018$

$Cp = \dfrac{U-L}{6\sigma} = \dfrac{0.0033 - 0.0023}{0.0018} = 0.555$

$Cpk = \dfrac{Z(min)}{3}$

$Z(U) = \dfrac{U-\overline{X}}{\sigma} = \dfrac{0.0033 - 0.0028}{0.0033} = 1.67$

$Z(L) = \dfrac{(\overline{X}-L)}{\sigma} = \dfrac{0.0028 - 0.0023}{0.0003} = 1.67$

$Cpk = \dfrac{1.67}{3} = 0.5555$

Process is centered but not capable of meeting specifications.

6.13 $\quad \sigma = \dfrac{\overline{s}}{c_4} = \dfrac{50}{0.8862} = 56$

$6\sigma = 336$

$Cp = \dfrac{U-L}{6\sigma} = \dfrac{550 - 250}{336} = 0.9$

$Cpk = \dfrac{Z(min)}{3}$ $\qquad$ X-bar = 390, n = 3

$Z(U) = \dfrac{U-\overline{X}}{\sigma} = \dfrac{550 - 390}{56} = 2.9$

$Z(L) = \dfrac{(\overline{X}-L)}{\sigma} = \dfrac{390 - 250}{56} = 0.7$

$Cpk = \dfrac{0.7}{3} = 0.23$

The process is nearly capable of meeting specifications but not centered.

6.14 $\quad \sigma = \dfrac{1.66}{2.059} = 0.81$

$6\sigma = 4.86$

$Cp = \dfrac{U-L}{6\sigma} = \dfrac{90 - 70}{6(0.81)} = 4.11$ Process is capable but not centered.

44

$$Cpk = \frac{Z(min)}{3}$$

$$Z(U) = \frac{U - \overline{X}}{\sigma} = \frac{90 - 73.58}{0.81} = 20.27$$

$$Z(L) = \frac{73.58 - 70}{0.81} = 4.42$$

$$Cpk = \frac{4.42}{3} = 1.47$$

6.15

Day	1	2	3	4	5
$\overline{\overline{X}}$	3.4794	3.7493	3.7492	3.7496	3.7503
Sigma	0.0048	0.0046	0.0036	0.0029	0.0008
6 Sigma	0.0288	0.0276	0.0216	0.0174	0.0048
Cp	0.3471	0.3623	0.463	0.5747	2.08
Cpk	0.3056	0.3116	0.389	0.529	1.958

Cp is the ratio that compares reality with customer wants. Cp tells whether or not the process is capable of meeting specifications. The Cpk ratio describes process centering.

6.16

$$Cpk = \frac{Z(min)}{3}$$

$$Z(U) = \frac{U - \overline{X}}{\sigma} = \frac{29 - 25}{1.18} = 3.39$$

$$Z(L) = \frac{25 - 21}{1.18} = 3.39$$

$$Cpk = \frac{3.39}{3} = 1.13 \quad \text{Process is centered.}$$

$$Cpk = \frac{Z(min)}{3}$$

$$Z(U) = \frac{U - \overline{X}}{\sigma} = \frac{55 - 45}{11.28} = 0.89$$

$$Z(L) = \frac{45 - 45}{11.28} = 0$$

$$Cpk = \frac{0}{3} = 0 \quad \text{Process average is equal to one of the specification limits.}$$

$$Cpk = \frac{Z(min)}{3}$$

$$Z(U) = \frac{U - \overline{X}}{\sigma} = \frac{82 - 77}{2.06} = 36$$

$$Z(L) = \frac{77 - 68}{2.06} = 4.4$$

$$Cpk = \frac{4.4}{3} = 1.46 \quad \text{Process is not centered.}$$

6.17   When Cp = Cpk +1.9, the process is centered and capable. The truck can be filled in the required time.

6.18 $$\sigma = \frac{1}{1.693} = 0.59$$

$$6\sigma = 3.54$$

$$Cp = \frac{U - L}{6\sigma} = \frac{17 - 13}{6(0.59)} = 1.13 \quad \text{Process is capable.}$$

$$Cpk = \frac{Z(min)}{3}$$

$$Z(U) = \frac{U - \overline{X}}{\sigma} = \frac{17 - 15}{0.59} = 3.39$$

$$Z(L) = \frac{15 - 13}{0.59} = 3.39$$

$$Cpk = \frac{3.39}{3} = 1.13 \quad \text{Process is centered.}$$

6.19 $$\sigma = \frac{0.009}{0.8862} = 0.01$$

$$6\sigma = 0.06$$

$$Cp = \frac{U - L}{6\sigma} = \frac{16.3 - 16.1}{6(0.01)} = 3.33 \quad \text{Process is capable but not centered.}$$

$$Cpk = \frac{Z(min)}{3}$$

$$Z(U) = \frac{U - \overline{X}}{\sigma} = \frac{16.3 - 16.242}{0.01} = 5.8$$

$$Z(L) = \frac{16.242 - 16.1}{0.01} = 14.2$$

$$Cpk = \frac{5.8}{3} = 1.93$$

6.20 $\quad \sigma = \dfrac{0.05}{2.059} = 0.024$

$6\sigma = 0.144$

$Cp = \dfrac{U - L}{6\sigma} = \dfrac{1.65 - 1.35}{6(0.024)} = 2.08$ Process is capable but not centered.

$Cpk = \dfrac{Z(min)}{3}$

$Z(U) = \dfrac{U - \overline{X}}{\sigma} = \dfrac{1.65 - 1.49}{0.024} = 6.67$

$Z(L) = \dfrac{1.49 - 1.35}{0.024} = 5.83$

$Cpk = \dfrac{5.83}{3} = 1.94$

Chapter 7

7.1 $\quad \overline{X} = \dfrac{\sum X}{g} = \dfrac{604}{25} = 24.16$ or 24 mm

$\overline{R} = \dfrac{\sum R}{g-1} = \dfrac{26}{24} = 1.08$ or 1 mm

$UCL_X = \overline{X} + 2.660\overline{R}$
$\qquad = 24 + 2.660(1) = 26.66$ or 27 mm

$LCL_X = \overline{X} - 2.660\overline{R}$
$\qquad = 24 - 2.660(1) = 21.34$ or 21 mm

$UCL_R = 3.267\overline{R} = 3.267$ mm

$LCL_R = 0\overline{R} = 0$

$\sigma = \dfrac{\overline{R}}{d_2} = \dfrac{1}{1.128} = 0.89$

7.2 $\quad \overline{X} = \dfrac{\sum X}{g} = \dfrac{149000}{19} = 7842$

$\overline{R} = \dfrac{\sum R}{g-1} = \dfrac{16000}{18} = 890$ or 900

$UCL_X = \overline{X} + 2.660\overline{R} = 10209$

$LCL_X = \overline{X} - 2.660\overline{R} = 5475$

$UCL_R = 3.267\overline{R} = 2940$

$LCL_R = 0\overline{R} = 0$

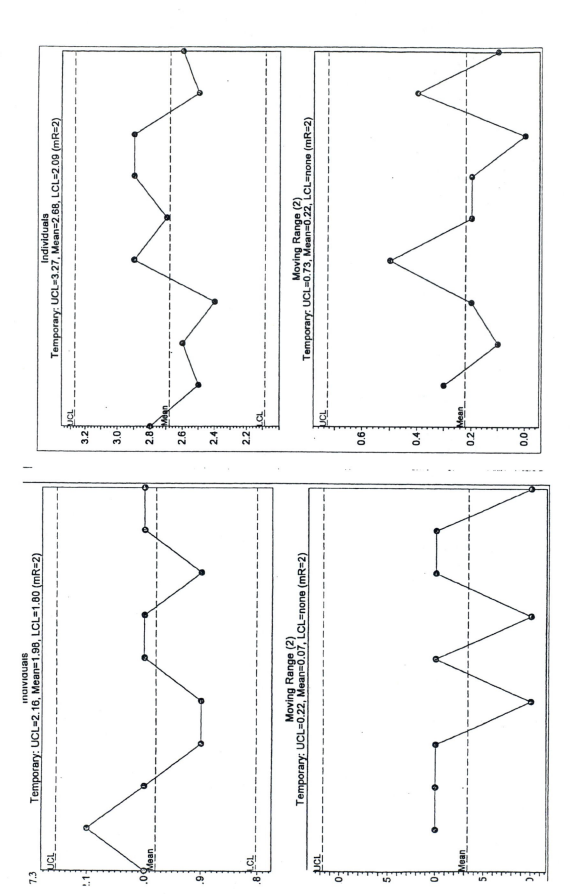

7.4

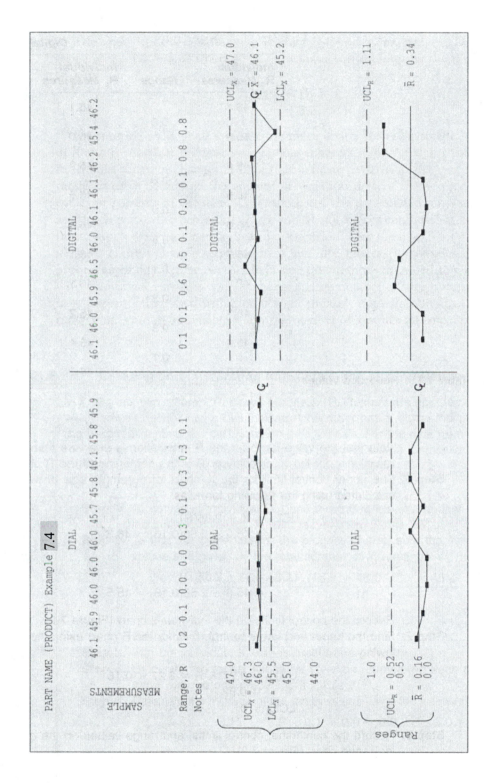

PART NAME (PRODUCT) Example 7.4

7.5

$$X\text{-bar} = \frac{720}{14} = 51$$

$$R\text{-bar} = \frac{198}{13} = 15$$

$$UCL_X = \overline{X} + 2.660\overline{R}$$
$$= 51 + 2.660(15) = 91$$
$$LCL_X = \overline{X} - 2.660\overline{R}$$
$$= 51 - 2.660(15) = 11$$

$$UCL_R = 3.267\overline{R} = 49$$
$$LCL_R = 0\overline{R} = 0$$

7.6

	Value	3 period Moving sum	$\overline{X}$	R
1	36	-		
2	35	-		
3	37	108	36	2
4	38	110	37	3
5	32	107	36	6
6	35	105	35	6
7	36	103	34	4
8	35	106	35	1
9	28	99	33	8
10	27	90	30	8
11	35	90	30	8
12	36	98	33	9
13	35	106	35	1
14	34	105	35	2
15	37	106	35	3

$$\frac{\sum \overline{X}}{g} = \frac{444}{13} \qquad \frac{\sum R}{g} = \frac{61}{13}$$

$$\overline{\overline{X}} = 34 \qquad \overline{R} = 5$$

$$UCL_X = \overline{\overline{X}} + A_2\overline{R} = 34 + (1.023)(5) = 39$$
$$LCL_X = \overline{\overline{X}} - A_2\overline{R} = 34 - (1.023)(5) = 29$$

$$UCL_R = D_4\overline{R} = (2.574)(5) = 13$$
$$LCL_R = D_3\overline{R} = (0)(5) = 0$$

7.7

n = 4

1	0.806	-		
2	0.814	-		
3	0.810	-		
4	0.820	3.250	0.813	0.014
5	0.819	3.263	0.816	0.010
6	0.815	3.264	0.816	0.010
7	0.817	3.271	0.818	0.005
8	0.810	3.261	0.815	0.009
9	0.811	3.253	0.813	0.007
10	0.809	3.247	0.812	0.008
11	0.808	3.238	0.810	0.003
12	0.810	3.238	0.810	0.003
13	0.812	3.239	0.810	0.004
14	0.810	3.240	0.810	0.004
15	0.809	3.241	0.810	0.003
16	0.807	3.238	0.810	0.005
17	0.807	3.233	0.808	0.003
18	0.808	3.231	0.808	0.002

$$\frac{\sum \overline{X}}{g} = \frac{12.179}{15} = 0.812 \qquad \frac{\sum R}{g} = \frac{0.09}{15} = 0.006$$

$$UCL_X = \overline{\overline{X}} + A_2 \overline{R} = 0.812 + (0.729)(0.006) = 0.816$$
$$UCL_X = \overline{\overline{X}} - A_2 \overline{R} = 0.812 - (0.729)(0.006) = 0.808$$

$$UCL_R = D_4 \overline{R} = (2.282)(0.006) = 0.014$$
$$LCL_R = D_3 \overline{R} = (0)(0.006) = 0$$

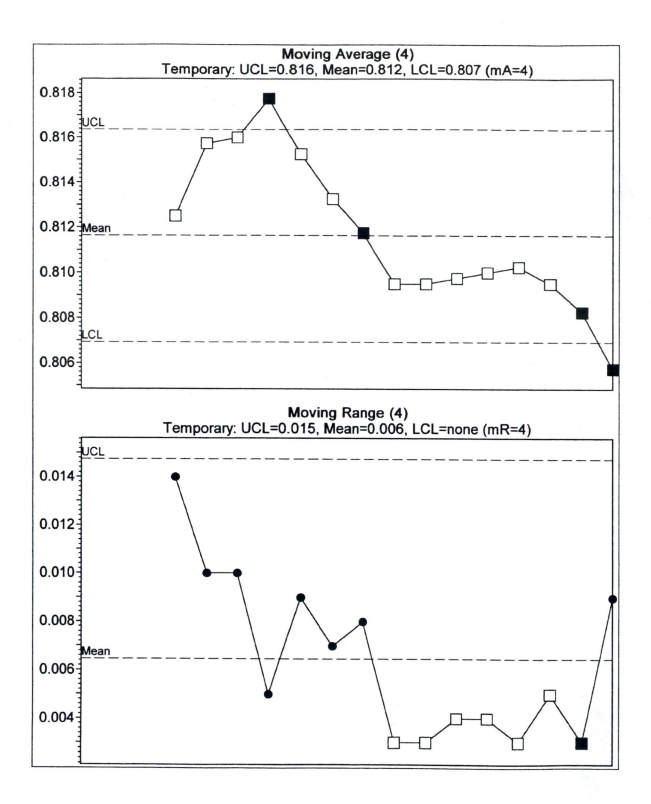

7.8

	Value	3 period Moving sum	$\overline{X}$	R
1	3650	-		
2	3550	-		
3	3700	10900	3533	150
4	3750	11000	3667	200
5	3900	11350	3783	200
6	3900	11550	3850	150
7	3850	11650	3883	50
8	3650	11400	3800	250
9	3650	11150	3717	200
10	3775	11075	3692	125
11	3700	11125	3708	125
12	3775	11250	3750	75
13	3900	11375	3792	200
14	3900	11575	3858	125
15	3800	11600	3867	100
16	3700	11400	3800	200
17	3900	11400	3800	200
18	3950	11550	3850	250
19	4000	11850	3950	100

$$\frac{\sum \overline{X}}{g} = \frac{64400}{17} \qquad \frac{\sum R}{g} = \frac{2700}{17}$$

$$\overline{\overline{X}} = 3788 \qquad \overline{R} = 159$$

$UCL_X = \overline{\overline{X}} + A_2\overline{R} = 3788 + (1.023)(159) = 3951$

$LCL_X = \overline{\overline{X}} - A_2\overline{R} = 3788 - (1.023)(159) = 3625$

$UCL_R = D_4\overline{R} = (2.574)(159) = 409$

$LCL_R = D_3\overline{R} = (0)(159) = 0$

7.9

$$X\text{-bar} = \frac{31753}{12} = 2646$$

$$R\text{-bar} = \frac{3490}{12} = 291$$

$UCL_X = 2646 + 1.023(291) = 2944$
$LCL_X = 2646 - 1.023(291) = 2348$

$UCL_R = 2.574(291) = 749$
$LCL_R = 0\overline{R} = 0$

7.10

$$\overline{\overline{X}} = \frac{\sum \overline{X}_i}{g} = \frac{1806}{60} = 30.1$$

$$\overline{R} = \frac{\sum R}{g-1} = \frac{205}{59} = 3.5$$

$UCL_X = \overline{\overline{X}} + A_2\overline{R} = 30.1 + 0.729(3.5) = 32.6 = 33$
$LCL_X = \overline{\overline{X}} - A_2\overline{R} = 30.1 - 0.729(3.5) = 27.5 = 28$
$UCL_R = D_4\overline{R} = (2.282)(3.5) = 8$
$LCL_R = D_3\overline{R} = (0)(3.5) = 0$

7.11

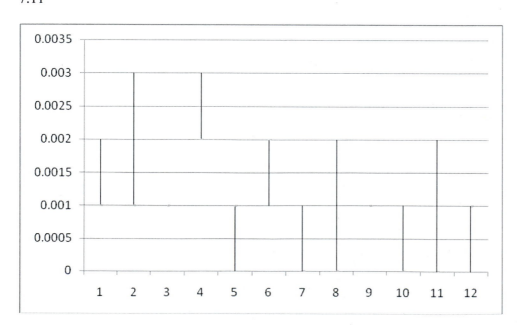

56

7.13

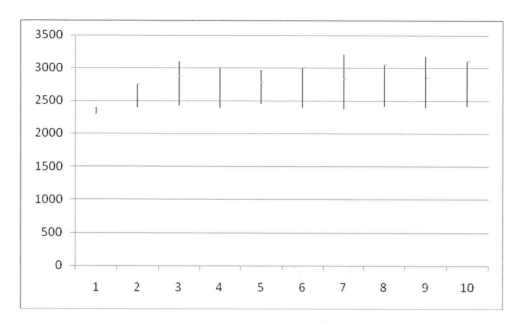

7.14 $\overline{X}md$ = 8.8 round to 9
        $\overline{R}md$ = 4.2 round to 4

        UCLmd = $\overline{X}md$ + A6$\overline{R}md$ = 9 + 1.19(4) = 13.76 = 13.76 or 14
        LCLmd = $\overline{X}md$ − A6$\overline{R}md$ = 9 − 1.19(4) = 4.24 or 4

        UCLr = D4$\overline{R}md$ = 2.575(4) = 10
        LCLr = D3$\overline{R}md$ = 0(4) = 0

7.15 $\overline{X}md$ = 73
        $\overline{R}md$ = 2

        UCLmd = $\overline{X}md$ + A6$\overline{R}md$ = 73 + 1.19(2) = 75
        LCLmd = $\overline{X}md$ − A6$\overline{R}md$ = 73 − 1.19(2) = 71

        UCLr = D4$\overline{R}md$ = 2.574(2) = 5
        LCLr = D3$\overline{R}md$ = 0(2) = 0

7.16 $\overline{X}md = 22$

   $\overline{R}md = 3.4$

   $UCLmd = \overline{X}md + A6\overline{R}md = 22 + 0.8(3.7) = 25$
   $LCLmd = \overline{X}md - A6\overline{R}md = 22 - 0.8(3.7) = 19$

   $UCLr = D4\overline{R}md = 2.282(3.7) = 8.4$
   $LCLr = D3\overline{R}md = 0(3.7) = 0$

7.17

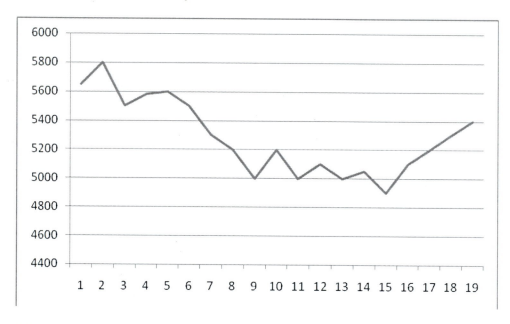

7.18

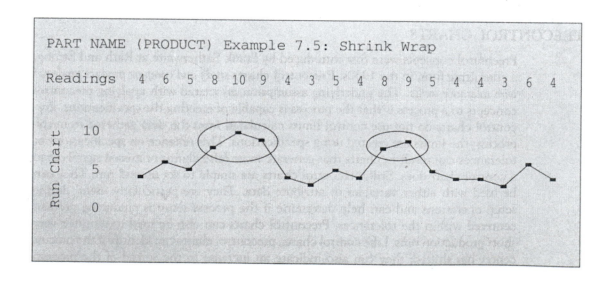

7.19

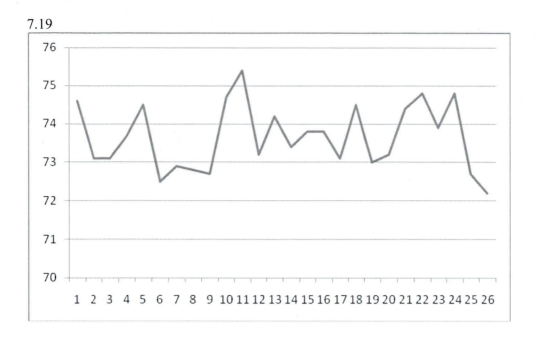

7.21 **Precontrol charts** *study and compare product produced with tolerance limits.* The underlying assumption associated with applying precontrol concepts to a process is that the process is capable of meeting the specifications. Precontrol charts do not use control limits calculated from the data gathered from the process; the limits are created using specifications. This reliance on specifications or tolerances can result in charts that generate more false alarms or missed signals than a control chart does. Create the zones. Place the upper and lower specification limits on the chart. Determine the center of the specification; this becomes the centerline on the chart. Create the zones by finding the center of area between the specification limits and the center of the tolerance. To do this, subtract the centerline from the upper specification limit, divide this value in half, and add the result to the centerline. To divide the lower half of the precontrol chart, subtract the lower specification limit from the centerline, divide this value in half, and subtract the result from the centerline.

7.22	MAX TOL	0.0020	
	1/2 MAX TOL	0.0015	
	NOMINAL	0.0010	
	1/2 MIN TOL	0.0005	
	MIN TOL	0.0000	
	0.0021	ADJUST	
	0.0013		
	0.0014		
	0.0007		
	0.0002	CHECK ANOTHER PIECE	
	0.0022	ADJUST	
	0.0021	ADJUST	
	0.0006		
	0.0010		
	0.0011		
	0.0014		
	0.0013		
	0.0010	RUN RULES	
	0.0012		
	0.0011		
	0.0013		
	0.0016		
	0.0015	CONTINUE	
	0.0015	CONTINUE	
	0.0014		
	0.0009		
	0.0012		
	0.0012		
	0.0012		
	0.0012		
	0.0014		
	0.0017	ADJUST	
	0.0020	RETURN TO PRECONTROL SET UP RULES	
	0.0021	ADJUST	
	0.0015		
	0.0012		
	0.0010		

7.23	MAX TOL	0.260
	1/2 MAX TOL	0.255
	NOMINAL	0.250
	1/2 MIN TOL	0.245
	MIN TOL	0.240

0.250	CONTINUE	
0.250	CONTINUE	
0.251	CONTINUE	
0.250	CONTINUE	
0.252	BEGIN RUNNING NORMAL PRODUCTION (RUN RULES)	
0.253		
0.252	CONTINUE	
0.255	GREEN	
0.259	YELLOW	CONTINUE
0.261	RED	ADJUST PROCESS
0.249	CONTINUE	
0.250	CONTINUE	
0.250	CONTINUE	
0.250	CONTINUE	
0.252	BEGIN RUNNING NORMAL PRODUCTION (RUN RULES)	
0.251	CONTINUE	
0.253	CONTINUE	
0.254	CONTINUE	
0.254	CONTINUE	
0.256	YELLOW	
0.259	YELLOW	ADJUST PROCESS; RETURN TO SETUP RULES
0.259	YELLOW	CHECK ANOTHER PIECE
0.260	YELLOW	ADJUST PROCESS
0.261	RED	ADJUST PROCESS
0.248	CONTINUE	
0.248	CONTINUE	

7.24   Nominal 0.2950

$\overline{X}1$	0.000125
$\overline{X}2$	−0.00005
$\overline{X}3$	−0.00015
$\overline{X}4$	−0.000075
$\overline{X}5$	−0.00015
$\overline{X}6$	0.00005
$\overline{X}7$	−0.000075

Nominal 0.6850

$\overline{X}8$	0.00005
$\overline{X}9$	0
$\overline{X}10$	0.00015
$\overline{X}11$	−0.000175
$\overline{X}12$	0.00005

Centerline = −0.00025/12 = −0.000021

UCLx = centerline + $A2\overline{R}$ = −0.000021 + (0.729)(0.0006) = 0.00042

LCLx = centerline − $A2\overline{R}$ = −0.000021 − (0.729)(0.0006) = −0.00046

$\overline{R}$ = 72/12 = 0.0006

UCLr = $D4\overline{R}$ = 2.282(0.0006) = 0.00137
LCLr = $D3\overline{R}$ = 0

7.25 $\overline{X} = 0.033$
$\overline{X} = 0.033$
$\overline{X} = -0.067$
$\overline{X} = 0.067$
$\overline{X} = 0.067$
$\overline{X} = 0.033$
$\overline{X} = -0.1$
$\overline{X} = 0.033$
$\overline{X} = 0.167$
$\overline{X} = 0.067$
$\overline{X} = 0.067$

$$\overline{\overline{X}} = \frac{0.4}{11} = 0.036 \qquad\qquad \overline{R} = \frac{1.9}{11} = 0.173$$

$UCL_X = 0.036 + (1.023)(0.173) = 0.213$
$LCL_X = 0.036 - (1.023)(0.173) = -0.141$

$UCL_R = (2.574)(0.173) = 0.45$
$LCL_R = (0)(0.173) = 0$

7.26
$$\overline{\overline{X}} = \frac{6.676}{21} = 0.32 \qquad\qquad \overline{R} = \frac{4.9}{21} = 0.23$$

$UCL_X = 0.32 + (0.577)(0.23) = 0.45$
$LCL_X = 0.32 - (0.577)(0.23) = 0.19$

$UCL_R = (2.114)(0.23) = 0.49$
$LCL_R = (0)(0.173) = 0$

Chapter 8

8.1   P(P) = 0.35
       P(B) = 0.46
       P(G) = 0.15
       P(P U R) = 0.04
       P(B or P U R) = 0.46 + 0.04 = 0.50

8.2 $P(\text{win prize}) = \dfrac{100}{12500} = 0.008$

8.3   P(orange and five) = 1/24
       P(orange)   = 6/24
       P(five)   = 3/24

8.4 $P_3^5 = \dfrac{5!}{(5-3)!} = \dfrac{120}{2} = 60$

8.5 $C_5^{15} = \dfrac{15!}{5!(15-5)!} = 3003$

       $P_5^{15} = \dfrac{15!}{(15-5)!} = 360{,}360$

8.6   P(Hayes)   = 0.75
       P(Romig)   = 0.25
       P(performs | Hayes)   = 0.95
       P(performs | Romig)   = 0.80
       P(P) = P(performs) = P(P and H) + P(p and R) = ?

       P(P and H) = P(P|H) · P(H) = 0.95(0.75) = 0.71
       P(P and R) = P(P|R) · P(R) = 0.80(0.25) = 0.20
       P(performs) = 0.71 + 0.20 = 0.91

8.7 $P(H|P) = \dfrac{P(P \text{ and } H)}{P(P)} = \dfrac{0.71}{0.91} = 0.78$

8.8   0.50 undergraduate
       0.25 graduate
       0.25 working

       0.05(0.50) + 0.01(0.25) + 0.01(0.25) = 0.03
       There is a 3% chance that an apartment has been damaged.

8.9 $P(\text{Fabric 1}) = \dfrac{460}{1000} = 46$

$P(\text{Fabric 2}|\text{Style 1}) = \dfrac{55}{305} = 0.18$

$P(\text{Style 4}) = \dfrac{255}{1000} = 0.255$

$P(\text{Style 3}|\text{Fabric 3}) = \dfrac{85}{365} = 0.23$

8.10   a. $P(\text{shipping}|\text{male}) = \dfrac{P(\text{shipping and male})}{P(\text{male})} = \dfrac{72/200}{120/200} = 0.6$

b. $P(\text{packing}|\text{male}) = \dfrac{P(\text{packing and male})}{P(\text{male})} = \dfrac{48/200}{120/200} = 0.4$

c. $P(\text{male and shipping}) = P(\text{male}) \times P(\text{shipping})$

$$\frac{72}{200} = \frac{120}{200} \times \frac{120}{200}$$

$0.36 = 0.36$

independent

8.11

$N = 15$
$D = 1$
$n = 3$
$d = 1$

$P(1) = \dfrac{\dfrac{1!}{1!0!} \times \dfrac{14!}{2!12!}}{\dfrac{15!}{3!12!}} = 0.20$

The manager has a 20% chance of finding the box containing blue paper within 3 randomly selected cases.

8.12

$N = 12$
$D = 2$
$n = 4$
$d = 2$

$P(2) = \dfrac{\dfrac{2!}{2!0!} \times \dfrac{10!}{2!8!}}{\dfrac{12!}{4!8!}} = 0.09$

The manager has a 9% chance of finding the cases which were dropped within 4 randomly selected cases.

8.13   P(2 or fewer) = P(0) + P(1) + P(2)

N = 10
D = 4
n = 3
d = 2, 1, 0

$$P(2) = \frac{\frac{4!}{2!2!} \times \frac{6!}{1!5!}}{\frac{10!}{3!7!}} = 0.30$$

N = 10
D = 4
n = 3
d = 2, 1, 0

$$P(1) = \frac{\frac{4!}{1!3!} \times \frac{6!}{2!4!}}{\frac{10!}{3!7!}} = 0.5$$

N = 10
D = 4
n = 3
d = 2, 1, 0

$$P(2) = \frac{\frac{4!}{0!4!} \times \frac{6!}{3!3!}}{\frac{10!}{3!7!}} = 0.17$$

P(2 or fewer) = P(2) + P(1) + P(0) = 0.3 + 0.5 + 0.17 = 0.97

The father has a 97% chance of finding the doll within three stores.

8.14

N = 10
D = 4
d = 2
n = 5
hypergeometric

$$\frac{\frac{4!}{2!2!} \times \left(\frac{6!}{3!3!}\right)}{\frac{10!}{5!5!}} = 0.476$$

P(1 or fewer) = P(1) + P(0) = 0.238 + 0.024 = 0.262

$$P(1) = \frac{\frac{4!}{1!3!} \times \left(\frac{6!}{4!2!}\right)}{\frac{10!}{5!5!}} = 0.238$$

$$P(0) = \frac{\frac{4!}{0!4!} \times \left(\frac{6!}{5!1!}\right)}{\frac{10!}{5!5!}} = 0.024$$

8.15

N = 15
D = 4
d = 1
n = 2

$$P(1) = \frac{\frac{4!}{1!3!} \times \left(\frac{11!}{1!10!}\right)}{\frac{15!}{2!13!}} = 0.419$$

8.17

N = 12
D = 3
d = 0
n = 2

$$P(0) = \frac{\frac{3!}{0!3!} \times \left(\frac{9!}{2!7!}\right)}{\frac{12!}{2!10!}} = 0.545$$

8.18

N = 10
D = 4
d = 3
n = 2

$$P(2) = \frac{\frac{4!}{2!2!} \times \left(\frac{6!}{1!5!}\right)}{\frac{10!}{3!7!}} = 0.300$$

8.19

N = 12
n = 3
d = 1
D = 1

$$P(1) = \frac{\frac{1!}{1!0!} \times \left(\frac{11!}{2!9!}\right)}{\frac{12!}{3!9!}} = 0.25$$

In three samples, there is a 25% probability of finding a non-conforming bag.

8.20

N = 20
n = 6
d = 4
D = 4

$$P(4) = \frac{\dfrac{4!}{4!\ 0!}\ \dfrac{16!}{2!\ 14!}}{\dfrac{20!}{6!\ 14!}} = 0.0031$$

In six samples, there is a 0.03% probability of finding all 4 infected animals.

8.21

N = 50
n = 10
d = 3
D = 15

$$P(3) = \frac{\dfrac{15!}{3!\ 12!}\ \dfrac{35!}{7!\ 28!}}{\dfrac{50!}{10!\ 40!}} = 0.30$$

In ten samples, there is a 30% probability of three of the 10 chips failing to meet specs.

8.22

N = 36
n = 8
d = 3
D = 6

$$P(3) = \frac{\dfrac{6!}{3!\ 3!}\ \dfrac{30!}{5!\ 25!}}{\dfrac{36!}{8!\ 28!}} = 0.094$$

In three samples, there is a 9.4% probability of finding three cookies that don't pass.

8.23

n = 6
P(1 or 0) = ?
p = 0.034
q = 0.966

$$P(0) = \frac{6!}{0!\,6!}(0.034)^0 (0.966)^6 = 0.81$$

$$P(1) = \frac{6!}{1!\,5!}(0.034)^1 (0.966)^5 = 0.17$$

$$P(1 \text{ or less}) = P(0) + P(1) = 0.81 + 0.17 = 0.98$$

8.24

p = 0.04
n = 15

$$P(1) = \frac{15!}{1!\,14!}(0.04)^1 (0.96)^{14} = 0.34$$

There is a 34% chance that one of the fifteen samples taken per day will contain an excessive amount of pollutants.

8.25

P(2)
p = 0.03
q = 0.97
n = 20

$$P(2) = \frac{20!}{2!\,18!}(0.03)^2 (0.97)^{18} = 0.10$$

8.26   P(more than 4) = 1 − P(4 or less) = 1 − [P(4) + P(3) + P(2) + P(1) = P(0)]

P(0) = 0.44
P(1) = 0.37
P(2) = 0.15
P(3) = 0.033
P(4) = 0.006

P(more than 4) = 1 − P(4 or less) = 1 − 0.9990 = 0.001

8.27

n = 6
p = 0.03
q = 0.97
P(2)

$$P(2) = \frac{6!}{2!\,4!}(0.03)^2 (0.97)^4 = 0.012$$

8.28

n = 10
p = 0.10
q = 0.90
P(5)

$$P(5) = \frac{10!}{5!\,5!}(0.10)^5(0.90)^5 = 0.0015$$

8.29

n = 6
p = 0.10
q = 0.90
P(more than 2) = 1 − P(2 or less)

$$P(2) = \frac{6!}{2!\,4!}(0.10)^2(0.90)^4 = 0.098$$

$$P(1) = \frac{6!}{1!\,5!}(0.10)^1(0.90)^5 = 0.354$$

$$P(0) = \frac{6!}{0!\,6!}(0.10)^0(0.90)^6 = 0.531$$

P(more than 2) = 1 − [0.098 + 0.354 + 0.531] = 1 − 0.983 = 0.017

8.30

n = 3
p = 0.25
q = 0.75
P(1 or less) = P(1) + P(0)

$$P(1) = \frac{3!}{1!\,2!}(0.25)^1(0.75)^2 = 0.42$$

$$P(0) = \frac{3!}{0!\,3!}(0.25)^0(0.75)^3 = 0.42$$

P(1 or less) = 0.42 + 0.42 = 0.84

8.31

n = 4
P(less than 2) = P(0) + P(1)
p = 0.05
q = 0.95
$$= \frac{4!}{0!\,4!}(0.05)^0(0.95)^4 + \frac{4!}{1!\,3!}(0.05)^1(0.95)^3$$
$$= 0.815 + 0.171$$
$$= 0.986$$

8.32

$n = 10$
$P(\text{2 or fewer}) = P(0) + P(1) + P(2)$
$p = 0.003$
$q = 0.997$

$$= \frac{10!}{0! \; 10!} (0.003)^0 (0.997)^{10} = 0.9704$$

$$= \frac{10!}{1! \; 9!} (0.003)^1 (0.997)^9 = 0.0292$$

$$= \frac{10!}{2! \; 8!} (0.003)^2 (0.997)^8 = 0.0004$$

$$= 0.9704 + 0.0292 + 0.0004$$

$$= 1.000$$

8.33

$n = 40$
$P(\text{1 or fewer}) = P(0) + P(1)$
$p = 0.005$
$q = 0.995$

$$= \frac{40!}{1! \; 39!} (0.005)^1 (0.995)^{39} = 0.1645$$

$$= \frac{40!}{0! \; 40!} (0.005)^0 (0.995)^{40} = 0.8183$$

$$= 0.1645 + 0.8183$$

$$= 0.9828$$

8.34 $n = 16$
$P(1)$
$p = 0.008$
$q = 0.992$

$$= \frac{16!}{1! \ 15!}(0.008)^1(0.992)^{15} = 0.1135$$

$$= 0.1135$$

8.35 $np = 0.9$
$P(\text{at least } 1$

$$P(0) = \frac{(0.9)^0}{0!}e^{-0.9} = 0.41$$

$$P(\text{at least } 1) = 1 - P(0) = 1 - 0.41 = 0.59$$

8.36 $np = 0.3/\text{min}$ so for five minutes $0.3 \times 5 = 1.5$
$P(3)$
$P(3 \text{ in } 5 \text{ min}) = ?$

$$P(3 \text{ in } 5 \text{ min}) = \frac{(15)^3}{e!}e^{-1.5} = 0.13$$

8.37 $np = 0.9$
$P(\text{more than } 1 \text{ call}) = 1 - [P(0) + P(1)]$

$$P(0) = \frac{(0.9)^0}{0!}e^{-0.9} = 0.41$$

$$P(1) = \frac{(0.9)^1}{1!}e^{-0.9} = 0.37$$

$$P(\text{more than } 1 \text{ call}) = 1 - [0.47 + 0.37] = 0.22$$

8.38 $np = 3$
$P(\text{more than } 2) = 1 - [P(0) + P(1) + P(2)]$

$$P(0) = \frac{(3)^0}{0!}e^{-3} = 0.05$$

$$P(1) = \frac{(3)^1}{1!}e^{-3} = 0.15$$

$$P(2) = \frac{(3)^2}{2!}e^{-3} = 0.22$$

$$P(\text{more than } 2) = 1 - 0.42 = 0.58$$

8.39 $P(5) = \dfrac{2^5}{5!}e^{-2} = 0.036$ There is a 3.6% chance that 5 bags will arrive at once.

8.40 np = 2.9

P(2 or fewer) = P(0) + P(1) + P(2)

$$P(2) = \frac{(2.9)^2}{2!} e^{-2.9} = 0.23$$

$$P(1) = \frac{(2.9)^1}{1!} e^{-2.9} = 0.16$$

$$P(0) = \frac{(2.9)^0}{0!} e^{-2.9} = 0.055$$

P(2 or fewer) = 0.23 + 0.16 + 0.055 = 0.445

8.41 np = 1.5

P(2 or more) = 1 - P(0) + P(1)

$$P(1) = \frac{(1.5)^1}{1!} e^{-1.5} = 0.335$$

$$P(0) = \frac{(1.5)^0}{0!} e^{-1.5} = 0.223$$

P(2 or more) = 1 – [0.223 + 0.335] = 0.442

8.42 np = 20

P(2 or fewer) = P(0) + P(1) + P(2)

$$P(2) = \frac{(20)^2}{2!} e^{-20} = 4.12 \times 10^{-7}$$

$$P(1) = \frac{(20)^1}{1!} e^{-20} = 4 \times 10^{-8}$$

$$P(0) = \frac{(20)^0}{0!}\, e^{-20} = 2 \times 10^{-9}$$

$$P(2 \text{ or fewer}) = 4.54 \times 10^{-7}$$

8.43 $np = 1$

$$P(2 \text{ or more}) = 1 - P(0) + P(1)$$

$$P(1) = \frac{(1)^1}{1!}\, e^{-1} = 0.37$$

$$P(0) = \frac{(1)^0}{0!}\, e^{-1} = 0.37$$

$$P(2 \text{ or more}) = 1 - [0.37 + 0.37] = 0.26$$

8.44 $M = 9.07$ kg
       $\sigma = 0.40$ kg

a. $Z = \dfrac{8.3 - 9.07}{0.4} = -1.925$
    Area = 0.0271
       2.71% of bikes will weigh below 8.3 kg

b. $Z = \dfrac{8.0 - 9.07}{0.4} = -2.675$
    $\text{Area}_1 = 0.00375$

    $Z = \dfrac{10.10 - 9.07}{0.4} = 2.575$
    $\text{Area}_2 = 0.9950$

    Area between 8.0 kg and 10.10 kg = 0.9950 − 0.00375 = 0.9913

8.46 $np = 6(0.10) = 0.6$
       P(more than 2) = 1 − P(2 or less)

from Poisson tables $\Rightarrow$ P(2 or less) = 0.977

P(more than 2) = 1 − 0.977 = 0.023

8.47   P(2) = ?

$np = 6(0.3) = 0.18$

$$P(2) = \frac{(0.18)^2}{2!} e^{-0.18} = 0.014$$

calculated with Binomial $\Rightarrow P(2) = 0.12$
calculated with Poisson $\Rightarrow P(2) = 0.14$

Approximation is not exact, due to small sample size.

8.48 $p = 0.04$
$n = 15$
$np = 0.6$

$$P(1) = \frac{(0.6)^1}{1!} e^{-0.6} = 0.33$$

For this problem, the Poisson distribution is a very good approximation of the binomial.

8.49 $P(4.5 < 5 < 5.5) = ?$

$X = np = 10(0.10) = 1$

$s = np(1 - np) = 0.9487$

$$Z(4.5) < 5 < Z(5.5)$$
$$\frac{4.5 - 1}{0.9487} < 5 < \frac{5.5 - 1}{0.9487}$$
$$3.69 < 5 < 4.74$$
$$0.9999 < P(5) < 1$$

$P(5) = 1 - 0.9999 = 0.0001$

Compared with 0.0015, not a good approximation.

Chapter 9

9.1 A common cause of variation is inherent in a process. A special cause arises due to special circumstances. Common and special causes exist in all processes and therefore, all charts.

9.2 To determine if a process is under control on an attribute chart, the guidelines presented in Chapter 5, Variables Charts, are used. When interpreting an attribute chart, trends toward zero are okay. Users of the charts should check to see why it happened and try to repeat it. The centerline of a p, u, or c chart is process capability.

9.3 $\sum n = 2500$

$\sum np = 5$

$\overline{P} = \dfrac{5}{2500} = 0.002$ process capability

$UCL_P = 0.002 + 3\sqrt{\dfrac{0.002(1 - 0.002)}{250}} = 0.010$

$LCL_P = 0.002 - 3\sqrt{\dfrac{0.002(1 - 0.002)}{250}} = 0$

9.4 $\sum n = 1500$

$\sum np = 101$

$\overline{P} = \dfrac{101}{1500} = 0.07$ process capability

$UCL_P = 0.07 + 3\sqrt{\dfrac{0.07(1 - 0.07)}{60}} = 0.17$

$LCL_P = 0.07 - 3\sqrt{\dfrac{0.07(1 - 0.07)}{60}} = 0$

9.5 $\sum n = 600$

$\sum np = 41$

$$\bar{P} = \frac{41}{600} = 0.068$$

$$UCL_P = 0.068 + 3\sqrt{\frac{0.068(1-0.068)}{20}} = 0.237$$

$$LCL_p = 0.068 - 3\sqrt{\frac{0.068(1-0.068)}{20}} = -0.100 \Rightarrow 0$$

9.6 $n = 200$

$\sum n = 2400$

$\sum np = 10$

$$\bar{P} = \frac{10}{2400} = 0.004$$

$$UCL_P = 0.004 + 3\sqrt{\frac{0.004(1-0.004)}{200}} = 0.0174$$

$$LCL_p = 0.004 - 3\sqrt{\frac{0.004(1-0.004)}{200}} = 0$$

9.7 $\sum n = 4500$

$\sum np = 173$

$$\bar{P} = \frac{173}{4500} = 0.038$$

$$UCL_P = 0.038 + 3\sqrt{\frac{0.038(1-0.038)}{150}} = 0.085$$

$$LCL_p = 0.038 - 3\sqrt{\frac{0.038(1-0.038)}{150}} = 0$$

9.8   n = 20

$$\overline{P} = \frac{120}{25(20)} = 0.24$$

$$UCL_P = 0.24 + 3\sqrt{\frac{0.24(1-0.24)}{20}} = 0.53$$

$$LCL_p = 0.24 - 3\sqrt{\frac{0.24(1-0.24)}{20}} = 0$$

One point out-of-control, fairly balanced otherwise, 2/3 of the points near the centerline, the points float freely back and forth across the centerline, no patterns.

9.10   np = 9061

$$\overline{P} = \frac{9061}{19627} = 0.46$$

$$nave = \frac{19627}{15} = 1309$$

$$UCL_P = 0.46 + 3\sqrt{\frac{0.46(1-0.46)}{1309}} = 0.50$$

$$LCL_p = 0.46 - 3\sqrt{\frac{0.46(1-0.46)}{1309}} = 0.42$$

Check points:

1983	n = 1354	Case II, point inside limits, n > nave. Must check limits.

$$UCL_p = 0.46 + 3\sqrt{\frac{0.46(1-0.46)}{1354}} = 0.50$$

1991	n = 1400	Case III, point outside limits, n > nave. n limits will be narrower, point is out for both, no need to check the control limits.
1992	n = 1181	Case I, point inside limits, n < nave. Limits using n will be wider, no need to check the control limits for this point.

9.11 $\sum n = 10{,}000$

$\sum np = 131$

$$\overline{P} = \frac{131}{10000} = 0.0131$$

$$UCL_P = 0.0131 + 3\sqrt{\frac{0.0131(1 - 0.0131)}{500}} = 0.028$$

$$LCL_p = 0.0131 - 3\sqrt{\frac{0.0131(1 - 0.0131)}{500}} = 0$$

9.12 $\sum n = 10{,}050$

$\sum np = 131$

$$\overline{P} = \frac{131}{10050} = 0.0131$$

when n = 400 $$UCL_{400} = 0.013 + 3\sqrt{\frac{0.013(1 - 0.013)}{400}} = 0.030$$

$$LCL_{400} = 0.013 - 3\sqrt{\frac{0.013(1 - 0.013)}{400}} = 0$$

when n = 450 $$UCL_{450} = 0.013 + 3\sqrt{\frac{0.013(1 - 0.013)}{450}} = 0.029$$

$$LCL_{450} = 0.013 - 3\sqrt{\frac{0.013(1 - 0.013)}{450}} = 0$$

when n = 500 $$UCL_{500} = 0.013 + 3\sqrt{\frac{0.013(1 - 0.013)}{500}} = 0.028$$

$$LCL_{500} = 0.013 - 3\sqrt{\frac{0.013(1 - 0.013)}{500}} = 0$$

when n = 550 $$UCL_{550} = 0.013 + 3\sqrt{\frac{0.013(1 - 0.013)}{550}} = 0.028$$

$$LCL_{550} = 0.013 - 3\sqrt{\frac{0.013(1 - 0.013)}{550}} = 0$$

when n = 600 $$UCL_{600} = 0.013 + 3\sqrt{\frac{0.013(1 - 0.013)}{600}} = 0.027$$

$$LCL_{600} = 0.013 - 3\sqrt{\frac{0.013(1 - 0.013)}{600}} = 0$$

9.12 continued

If worked with nave:

nave = 503

$$UCL_p = 0.0131 + 3\sqrt{\frac{0.013(1-0.013)}{503}} = 0.028$$

Check points:

Point 1	n = 500	Case I, point inside limits, n < nave. Limits using n will be wider, no need to check the control limits for this point.
	p = 0.026	
Point 12	n = 400	Case IV, point outside limits, n > nave. n limits will be wider, check limits for this point.
	p = 0.030	

$$UCL_p = 0.0131 + 3\sqrt{\frac{0.013(1-0.013)}{400}} = 0.030$$

Point is on control limit. May or may not be signaling need to check process.

9.13 $n_{ave} = 2685$

$$\sum n = 32{,}222$$

$$\sum np = 595$$

$$\overline{P} = \frac{595}{32222} = 0.0185$$

$$UCL_{\overline{p}} = 0.0185 + 3\sqrt{\frac{0.0185(1-0.0185)}{2685}} = 0.0263$$

$$LCL_{\overline{p}} = 0.0185 - 3\sqrt{\frac{0.0185(1-0.0185)}{2685}} = 0.0107$$

check points 2, 3, 4, 9, 11

Run 2 $n_{ave} = 2685$
              $n = 2056$
              $n < n_{ave}$

- point 2: 0.041 out of control
- control limits will be wider for individual sample
- calculate limits

$$UCL_{2056} = 0.0185 + 3\sqrt{\frac{0.0185(1-0.0185)}{2056}} = 0.0274$$

point out of control for both n and n_{ave}

Run 3 $n_{ave} = 2685$
               $n = 2750$
               $n > n_{ave}$
        - point 3: 0.028 out of control
        - control limits will be narrower for individual sample
        - no need to calculate limits
               point out for both n and n_{ave}

Run 4 $n_{ave} = 2685$
               $n = 3069$
               $n > n_{ave}$
        - point 4: 0.035 out of control
        - control limits will be narrower for individual sample
        - no need to calculate limits
               point out for both n and n_{ave}

Run 9 $n_{ave} = 2685$
               $n = 2060$
               $n < n_{ave}$
        - point 9: 0.023 near limits of n_{ave}
        - control limits will be wider for individual sample
        - no need to calculate limits
               point in control for both n and n_{ave}

Run 11 $n_{ave} = 2685$
               $n = 2620$
               $n < n_{ave}$
        - point 11: 0.033 out of control
        - control limits will be wider for individual sample
        - must recalculate limits

$$UCL_{2620} = 0.0185 + 3\sqrt{\frac{0.0185(1-0.0185)}{2620}} = 0.0264$$

point out of control for both n and n_{ave}

9.14 $\quad \sum n = 660$

$\quad \sum np = 138$

$$n_{ave} = \frac{660}{22} = 30$$

$$\overline{P} = \frac{138}{660} = 0.21 \text{ process capability}$$

$$UCL_P = 0.21 + 3\sqrt{\frac{0.21(1-0.21)}{30}} = 0.43$$

$$LCL_P = 0.21 - 3\sqrt{\frac{0.21(1-0.21)}{30}} = 0$$

check points 18, 19, 21

Run 18
$\quad n_{ave} = 30$
$\quad n = 31$
$\quad n > n_{ave}$
- point 18: 0.42
- control limits will be narrower for individual sample
- calculate limits

$$UCL_P = 0.21 + 3\sqrt{\frac{0.21(1-0.21)}{31}} = 0.43 \text{ point inside limits}$$

Run 19
$\quad n_{ave} = 30$
$\quad n = 29$
$\quad n < n_{ave}$
- point 19: 0.79 out of control
- control limits will be narrower for n average
- calculate limits

$$UCL_P = 0.21 + 3\sqrt{\frac{0.21(1-0.21)}{29}} = 0.43 \text{ point out for both n and } n_{ave}$$

Run 21
$\quad n_{ave} = 30$
$\quad n = 34$
$\quad n > n_{ave}$
- point 21: 0.38 out of control
- control limits will be narrower for individual sample
- calculate limits

$$UCL_P = 0.21 + 3\sqrt{\frac{0.21(1-0.21)}{34}} = 0.42 \text{ point inside limits}$$

9.15 $\sum n = 660$

$\sum np = 138$

$n_{ave} = \dfrac{660}{22} = 30$

$\overline{P} = \dfrac{138}{660} = 0.21$ process capability

$UCL_P = 0.21 + 3\sqrt{\dfrac{0.21(1-0.21)}{30}} = 0.43$

$LCL_P = 0.21 - 3\sqrt{\dfrac{0.21(1-0.21)}{30}} = 0$

check points 3, 8, 19, 21

Run 3 $n_{ave} = 30$
               $n = 31$
               $n > n_{ave}$
          - point 18: 0.55
          - control limits will be narrower for individual sample
          - no need to calculate limits

Run 8 $n_{ave} = 30$
               $n = 31$
               $n > n_{ave}$
          - point 18: 0.42
          - control limits will be narrower for individual sample
          - calculate limits

$UCL_P = 0.21 + 3\sqrt{\dfrac{0.21(1-0.21)}{31}} = 0.43$ point inside limits

Run 19 $n_{ave} = 30$
               $n = 29$
               $n < n_{ave}$
          - point 19: 0.79 out of control
          - control limits will be narrower for n average
          - calculate limits

$UCL_P = 0.21 + 3\sqrt{\dfrac{0.21(1-0.21)}{29}} = 0.43$ point out for both n and n_{ave}

Run 21 $n_{ave} = 30$
                $n = 34$
                $n > n_{ave}$
        - point 21: 0.38 out of control
        - control limits will be narrower for individual sample
        - calculate limits

$$UCL_P = 0.21 + 3\sqrt{\frac{0.21(1 - 0.21)}{34}} = 0.42 \quad \text{point inside limits}$$

9.17 $np = 50(0.09) = 4.5$

$$UCL_{np} = 4.5 + 3\sqrt{4.5(1 - 0.09)} = 11$$
$$LCL_{np} = 4.5 - 3\sqrt{4.5(1 - 0.09)} = 0$$

9.18 $\bar{p} = \dfrac{2.32}{25} = 0.09 \times 100\% = 9\%$

$$UCL_\% = 0.09 + 3\sqrt{\frac{(0.09)(1 - 0.09)}{25}} = 0.021 \times 100\% = 21\%$$

$$LCL_\% = 0.09 - 3\sqrt{\frac{(0.09)(1 - 0.09)}{25}} = 0$$

9.19 $\sum n = 12000$
        $\sum np = 84$

$$\bar{P} = \frac{84}{12000} = 0.007$$

$$np = \frac{84}{12} = 7 \quad \text{process capability}$$

$$UCL_P = 7 + 3\sqrt{7(1 - 0.007)} = 15$$

$LCL_P = 0$

This process shows a jump in level after point 5.

9.20 $\overline{np} = \dfrac{\sum np}{m} = \dfrac{300}{25} = 12$

$\overline{p} = \dfrac{\sum np}{\sum n} = \dfrac{300}{25(100)} = 0.12$

$UCL_{np} = 12 + 3\sqrt{12(1-0.12)} = 22$

$LCL_{np} = 12 - 3\sqrt{12(1-0.12)} = 2$

One point beyond upper control limit. 2/3 of points are near the centerline. A few points are on or close to the centerline. The points are balanced and they float back and forth across the centerline.

9.21 $\sum n = 220$

$\sum np = 158$

$\overline{P} = \dfrac{158}{220} = 0.07$

$np = \dfrac{158}{22} = 7$ process capability

$UCL_P = 7 + 3\sqrt{7(1-0.07)} = 11$

$LCL_P = 7 + 3\sqrt{7(1-0.07)} = 3$

9.22 $\sum n = 160$

$\sum np = 10$

$\overline{P} = \dfrac{10}{160} = 0.0625$

$np = \dfrac{10}{20} = 0.5$ process capability

$UCL_P = 0.5 + 3\sqrt{0.5(1-0.0625)} = 2.56$

$LCL_P = 0.5 + 3\sqrt{0.5(1-0.0625)} = 0$

9.23 $\sum np = 198$

$\sum n = 2400$

$\overline{P} = \dfrac{198}{2400} = 0.0825$

$\overline{np} = \dfrac{198}{15} = 13$

$UCL_{np} = 13 + 3\sqrt{13(1-0.0825)} = 23$

$LCL_{np} = 13 - 3\sqrt{13(1-0.0825)} = 3$

9.24 $\sum np = 243$

$\sum n = 6000$

$\overline{P} = \dfrac{243}{6000} = 0.0405$

$\overline{np} = \dfrac{243}{20} = 12$ process capability is centerline $\overline{np} = 12$

$UCL_{np} = 12 + 3\sqrt{12(1-0.0405)} = 22$

$LCL_{np} = 12 - 3\sqrt{12(1-0.0405)} = 2$

9.25 $\sum np = 104$

$\sum n = 8000$

$\overline{P} = 0.013$

$\overline{np} = \dfrac{104}{20} = 5$

$UCL_{np} = 5 + 3\sqrt{5(1-0.013)} = 12$

$LCL_{np} = 5 - 3\sqrt{5(1-0.013)} = 0$

9.26 $\overline{c} = 8$

$UCL_c = 8 + 3\sqrt{8} = 16$

$LCL_c = 8 - 3\sqrt{8} = 0$

Will not meet customer specifications because process capability is currently 8, twice the value specified by the customer.

9.27 $\bar{c} = \dfrac{\sum c}{m} = \dfrac{27}{5} = 1$

$UCL_c = 1 + 3\sqrt{1} = 4$
$LCL_c = 1 - 3\sqrt{1} = 0$

Line can not meet specifications. The level of defects is slightly above 1.

9.28 $\bar{c} = \dfrac{6}{10} = 0.6$ process capability

$UCL_c = 0.6 + 3\sqrt{0.6} = 3$
$LCL_c = 0.6 - 3\sqrt{0.6} = 0$

The process capability is 0.6. The process is stable and under control.

9.29 $\bar{c} = \dfrac{142}{24} = 6$ process capability

$UCL_c = 6 + 3\sqrt{6} = 13$
$LCL_c = 6 - 3\sqrt{6} = 0$

The process capability is 6. The process exhibits an upward trend.

9.30 $\bar{c} = 5$

$UCL_c = 5 + 3\sqrt{5} = 11$
$LCL_c = 5 - 3\sqrt{5} = 0$

Since the centerline, $\bar{c}$, is five, the process is not capable.

9.31 $\bar{c} = \dfrac{11373}{22} = 517$ process capability

$UCL_c = 517 + 3\sqrt{517} = 585$
$LCL_c = 517 - 3\sqrt{517} = 449$

The process capability is 517, the average cost of future medical claims. The process is stable and under control. The highest expected costs are 585, the upper control limit.

9.32 $\sum c = 113$

$$\bar{c} = \frac{113}{20} = 6$$

$$UCL_c = 6 + 3\sqrt{6} = 13$$
$$LCL_c = 6 - 3\sqrt{6} = 0$$

9.33 $\bar{u} = \dfrac{\sum c}{\sum n} = \dfrac{469}{200} = 2.345$

$$UCL_u = 2.345 + 3\sqrt{\frac{2.345}{20}} = 3$$
$$LCL_u = 2.345 - 3\sqrt{\frac{2.345}{20}} = 1$$

9.34 $n = 400$

$$\bar{u} = \frac{\sum c}{\sum n} = \frac{780}{8000} = 0.098$$

$$UCL_u = 0.098 + 3\sqrt{\frac{0.098}{400}} = 0.145$$
$$LCL_u = 0.098 - 3\sqrt{\frac{0.098}{400}} = 0.051$$

9.35 $\bar{u} = \dfrac{\sum c}{\sum n} = \dfrac{2388}{2025} = 1.18$

$$UCL_u = 1.18 + 3\sqrt{\frac{1.18}{101}} = 1.5$$
$$LCL_u = 1.18 - 3\sqrt{\frac{1.18}{101}} = 0.86$$

9.36 $\quad \bar{u} = \dfrac{\sum c}{\sum n} = \dfrac{2388}{2025} = 1.18$ process capability

$n_{ave} = 100$

$UCL_u = 1.18 + 3\sqrt{\dfrac{1.18}{100}} = 1.51$

$LCL_u = 1.18 - 3\sqrt{\dfrac{1.18}{100}} = 0.85$

The process capability is 1.18. The process is stable and under control.

April 21 nave = nind = 100 no need to test. Point in control.

April 27 nave > nind 100 > 88, no need to test. Point in control.

No points out of control, so no tests for Case III or IV.

9.37 $\quad nave = \dfrac{\sum n}{m} = \dfrac{660}{22} = 30$

$\bar{P} = \dfrac{\sum np}{\sum n} = \dfrac{138}{660} = 0.21$

$UCL_p = 0.21 + 3\dfrac{\sqrt{(0.21)(1-0.21)}}{\sqrt{30}} = 0.433$

$LCL = 0$

Case II

Pt. 18: 31 > 30   0.42 < 0.43 $\qquad$ Calculate limits

$UCL_p = 0.21 + 3\dfrac{\sqrt{(0.21)(1-0.21)}}{\sqrt{31}} = 0.43$ point inside limits

Pt. 21: 34 > 30   0.38 < 0.43

$UCL_p = 0.21 + 3\dfrac{\sqrt{(0.21)(1-0.21)}}{\sqrt{34}} = 0.42$ point inside limits

Case III

Pt. 3: $31 > 30$ $0.55 > 0.433$ point outside for both nind and nave

Case IV

Pt. 19: $29 < 30$ $0.79 > 0.433$ Calculate limits

$$UCL_p = 0.21 + 3\frac{\sqrt{(0.21)(1 - 0.21)}}{\sqrt{29}} = 0.44$$

Chapter 10

10.1   Reliability is Quality in the long term. The ability of a product or service to perform its intended function in its designed conditions.

10.3   The life history curve has three distinct phases. The early failure phase is characterized by a larger number of failures, usually due to poor design or manufacturing. The second phase extends during the normal useful life of the product. Very few failures occur during this time. As a product ages, the number of failures increases.

10.5   Traffic signal reliability. Critical to the definition is the ability of the traffic signal to perform its intended function (consistently and correctly signal traffic) over a period of time (how long should the traffic signal last in years) under prescribed environmental conditions (rain, sleet, snow, ice, sun, wind, etc.).

10.6   Testing the metal clip and latch system will require cycle dependent testing because the manufacturer will want to know how many times the mechanism can be expected to latch and unlatch correctly.

10.7   Tornado siren reliability. Critical to the definition is the ability of the tornado siren to perform its intended function (consistently and correctly signal bad weather) over a period of time (how long should the tornado siren last in years) under prescribed environmental conditions (rain, sleet, snow, ice, sun, wind, etc.).

10.8 $\lambda = \dfrac{\text{\# of failures}}{\text{sum of test times}} = \dfrac{4}{80 + 150 + 350 + 465 + 21(500)} = 0.00035$

$\theta = 2857$ hours

10.9 $\lambda = \dfrac{\text{\# of failures}}{\text{sum of test times}} = \dfrac{2}{45 + 72 + 10(90)} = 0.002$

$\theta = 500$ hours

10.10 $\lambda = \dfrac{2}{8(8776) + 2460 + 5962} = 0.0000254$

$\theta = 39{,}315$ hours average life before breakdown

$\text{Availability} = \dfrac{39315}{39{,}315 + 120} = 99.7$

10.11 $\lambda = \dfrac{2}{40 + 65 + 80 + 89 + 16(100)} = 0.002$

$\theta = 468.5$ hours average life before breakdown

10.12 $\quad \lambda = \dfrac{4}{20(200) + 91 + 103 + 145 + 155} = 0.0009$

10.13 $\quad \theta = \dfrac{8(1825) + 1575 + 960}{2} = 8567.5 \text{ hours}$

10.14 $\quad \theta = \dfrac{10(100) + 28 + 36 + 45 + 54 + 78}{5} = 248 \text{ hours}$

10.15 Parallel system is more reliable because only one of its components has to be working properly for the system to function. Series system requires all components to work.

10.16 $\quad R_s = RA *[RB + RE(1 - RB)] *[1 - (1 - RC)(1 - RD)]$
$R_s = 0.99 * [0.98 + 0.98(1 - 0.98)] * [1 - (1 - 0.94)(1 - 0.95)]$
$R_s = 0.99 * 0.9996 * 0.997$
$R_s = 0.987$

10.17 $\quad .99 \cdot [1 - (1 - .89)(1 - .89)] \cdot .98 \cdot [.95 + .95(1 - .95)]$
$0.99 \cdot 0.9879 \cdot 0.98 \cdot 0.9975$
$R_s = 0.9561$

10.18 $\quad .99 \cdot [1 - (1 - .98)(1 - .97)] \cdot [.95 + .93(1 - .95)] \cdot [1 - (1 - .98)(1 - .95)(1 - .96)]$
$0.99 \cdot 0.9994 \cdot 0.9965 \cdot 0.99996$
$R_s = 0.9859$

10.19 $\quad R_s = [R_g + R_b(1 - R_g)] * [1 - (1 - R_c)(1 - \{R_d * (1 - (1 - R_{ps})(1 - R_{lb})\}]$
$\qquad * [1 - (1 - R_{wd})(1 - R_{wd})(1 - R_{wd})]$
$R_s = [0.98 + 0.87(1 - 0.98)] * [1 - (1 - 0.95)(1 - \{0.95 * (1 - (1 - 0.90)(1 - 0.90)\}]$
$\qquad * [1 - (1 - 0.85)(1 - 0.85)(1 - 0.85)]$
$R_s = 0.9974 * 0.9970 * 0.9966$
$R_s = 0.991$

10.20

$[1 - (1 - .98)(1 - .98)] \cdot [.75 + .75 (1 - .75)] \cdot .96$
$0.9996 \cdot 0.9375 \cdot 0.96$
$R_s = 0.8996$

92

10.21 $0.8996 + .95(1 - .8996)$
       $R_s = 0.9950$

10.22 $R_s = 0.95 * [1 - (1 - 0.90)(1 - 0.90)] * [0.97 + 0.90(1 - 0.97)]$
              $* [1 - (1 - 0.80)(1 - 0.80)] * 0.95$
       $R_s = 0.95 * 0.99 * 0.997 * 0.96 * 0.95$
       $R_s = 0.855$
       The system will be operational 85.5% of the time.

10.23 $R(system) = 0.99 \times 0.98 \times 0.99 \times 0.97 \times [1 - (1 - 0.9215)(1 - 0.9215)] = 0.926$
       The system will be operational 92.6% of the time.

10.24 $R(system) = 0.80 \times [1 - (1 - 0.414)(1 - 0.238)] = 0.442$
       The system will be operational 44.2% of the time.

10.25 $R(system) = [0.98 + 0.75(1 - 0.98)] * [1 - (1 - 0.90)(1 - 0.90)(1 - 0.90)] * 0.92 * 0.96*0.85*$
       $[0.70 + 0.60(1 - 0.70)] * 0.95$
       $R(system) = 0.995 \times 0.999 \times 0.92 \times 0.96 \times 0.85 \times 0.88 \times 0.95 = 0.62$
       The system will be operational 62% of the time.

10.26 $R(system) = 0.98 *[0.95 + 0.85(1 - 0.95)] * [1 - (1 - 0.70)(1 - 0.60)]$
       $R(system) = 0.98 \times 0.9925 \times 0.88 = 0.86$
       The system will be operational 86% of the time.

Chapter 11

11.1 See Figure 11.1

11.2 QFD begins with the customer. Surveys and focus groups are used to gather information from the customers about their wants, needs, and expectations. Several key areas that should be investigated include performance, features, reliability, conformance, durability, serviceability, aesthetics, and perceived quality. Once this information is organized into a matrix, the customers are contacted to rate the importance of each of the identified wants and needs. Information is also gathered about how customers rate the company's product or service against the competition. Following this input form from the customers, technical requirements are developed. Once the matrix is constructed, the areas that need to be emphasized in the design of the product or service will be apparent.

11.3 Two of the main benefits of QFD are the reduced number of engineering changes and fewer production problems. A QFD provides key action items for improving customer satisfaction. A QFD can enable the launch of a new product or service to go more smoothly because customer issues and expectations have been dealt with in advance. Gathering and utilizing the voice of the customer is critical to the success of world class companies.

11.4
Factors	Levels
Supplier	A, B
Size	2" 3"
Plating	Yes, No

11.5 Define the components.
Factors: Supplier, Size, Plating
Levels:
	Factors	Levels
	Supplier	A, B
	Size	2" 3"
	Plating	Yes, No

Effect: Bending strength, when does the part fail?
Response Variable: Bending strength
Treatment: an arrangement of the factors at chosen levels: Supplier A,
Size 2" and Plating
Degrees of Freedom $(2 \times 2 \times 2) - 1 = 7$
Interaction may occur between any one or all of the factors.
Run: the application of one treatment to one experiment: Supplier B, Size 2", no plating.
Replicate: repeat one treatment
Significance: does the size, plating or supplier matter to bending strength.

11.6 Full-factorial experiment:
A, 2, Plating
A, 3, Plating
A, 2, No Plating
A, 3, No Plating
B, 2, Plating
B, 3, Plating
B, 2, No Plating
B, 3, No Plating

11.7	Factors	Levels
	Temp	250, 275, 300
	Time	5, 7, 9 sec
	Pressure	200, 250, 300 psi

11.8	Factors	Levels
	Temp	250, 275, 300
	Time	5, 7, 9 sec
	Pressure	200, 250, 300 psi

The effect, or response variable is part strength.

Treatment: Temperature 250, Time in mold 7 seconds, Pressure 300 psi

Degrees of Freedom $(3 \times 3 \times 3) - 1 = 26$

Interaction between temperature, time or pressure.

Significance: do any of these items (temp., time, Pressure) matter to the part strength?

11.9

Temp	Time	Pressure
250	5	200
250	7	200
250	9	200
250	5	250
250	7	250
250	9	250
250	5	300
250	7	300
250	9	300
275	5	200
275	7	200
275	9	200
275	5	250
275	7	250
275	9	250
275	5	300
275	7	300
275	9	300
300	5	200
300	7	200
300	9	200
300	5	250
300	7	250
300	9	250
300	5	300
300	7	300
300	9	300

11.10   Tire pressure and vehicle speed have no effect on gas mileage.

11.11   One error happens when you think something is true but it is not. The other error happens when you think something is not true when it is.

11.12

FACTORS	LEVEL 1	LEVEL 2
Width	18	24
Shelving	Flat	Angled
Line	Straight	Curved

The response variable being investigated is throughput time, the time to assemble and pack the items.

11.13   Failure Modes and Effects Analysis (FMEA) is a systematic approach to identifying both the ways that a product, part, process, or service can fail and the effects of those failures. Once identified, these potential failure modes are rated by the severity of their effects and the probability the failure will occur. FMEA is an effective error or failure prevention technique. FMEA's generate a list of potential failures, rank the critical characteristics, and generate to a list of actions that can be taken to eliminate the causes of failures or at least reduce their rate of occurrence. FMEA's are critical in the design of any system, process, service, or product, especially since they help identify potential failure modes that may adversely affect safety or government regulation compliance. Moreover, they identify these problems before the process or system is used or the product is put into production. Organizations utilizing FMEA improve the quality and reliability of their products, services, and processes.

11.14   **Systems FMEA**

A systems FMEA focuses on the big picture in order to optimize system designs whether for services or manufacturing industries. The system is studied in order to determine the possible ways the system can fail. Subsystems are also scrutinized. System FMEA's study the functions of the system in order to determine whether or not design deficiencies exist. System FMEA's also study the interactions of the system with other systems as well as how subsystems within the system interact with each other.

Process FMEA

Process FMEA's assist in the design or redesign of manufacturing, assembly, or service processes. Process FMEA's identify the different ways that a process fails and the effects of those failures. With this information, processes can be changed, controls can be developed, or detection methods put into place that will eliminate the possibility of process failure. Because they focus on potential process deficiencies, process FMEA's are often used to identify and rank process improvement opportunities.

Design FMEA

Design FMEA's focus on products. Often used during the product development stage, design FMEA's seek to identify potential product failure modes and the likelihood of those failures occurring. Design FMEA's assist in evaluating product design requirements and alternatives. They identify design deficiencies. They alert manufacturers to potential safety concerns.

11.15   Creating an FMEA

Begin by using a form similar to the one shown in Figure 16.1.
Users brainstorm potential failure modes, causes, effects, and probabilities of occurrence.

FMEA's begin with the study of the system, process, or part. This information is listed under item and function. For each item, when determining potential failure modes, ask these types of questions:

How can this system (process, service, part) fail to perform its intended function?
How would it be recognized that it didn't perform its intended function?
What could go wrong?
How would it be recognized that something has gone wrong?

When determining potential failure causes, ask these types of questions:

What might have triggered this reaction in the system (process, service, part)?
What factors need to be in place to cause this failure to occur in the system (process, service, part)?
What would cause this system (process, service, part) to fail in this manner?
Under what circumstances would this system (process, service, part) fail to perform its intended function?
What can cause this system (process, service, part) to fail to deliver its intended function?

When determining potential failure effects, ask these types of questions:

If the system (process, service, part) fails, what will be the consequences on the operation, function, or status of the system (process, part)?
If the system (process, service, part) fails, what will be the consequences on the operation, function, or status of the related systems (processes, service, parts)?
If the system (process, service, part) fails, what will be the consequences for the customer?
If the system (process, service, part) fails, what will be the consequence on government regulations?

Existing countermeasures answer the questions:

How will this cause of failure be recognized?
How can this cause of failure be prevented?
How can this cause of failure be minimized?
How can this cause of failure be mitigated?.

Severity ratings can range from 'no effect' to 'hazardous effect'. How many severity ratings used in an FMEA is up to those creating it. Figure 16.3 provides examples of severity ratings. The probability of occurrence can rank from 'impossible' to 'almost certain'.
A Risk Priority Number is the product of the severity rating and the probability of occurrence. Items with RPN's of one are dealt with first. An FMEA concludes with recommended actions. Starting with items with a RPN equal to one, these actions are designed to reduce the chance of failure occurring as well as the consequences associated with failure. These recommendations will include responsibilities, target completion dates, and reporting requirements for the actions taken.

11.21

					Failure Modes and Effects Analysis				
System (Process, Sevice, Part)			Food Preparation Area						
Team	Jim, Norm, Peg		Date 4/15/06						
Item	Function	Potential Failure Modes	Potential Causes	Failure Effect	Existing Controls, Counter measures Detection Methods	Probability	Severity	Risk Priority Code	Recommended Action, Responsibility, Target Date
Ventilation System Exhaust Fans	Maintain Quality of Air	Electrical: Power Short	faulty wiring, crossed wiring, damaged insulation	Unacceptable level of toxins in air causing eye and skin irritation, lung and brain damage.	Smoke Detector	occassional	critical	2	Investigate design of exhaust electrical system
	Maintain Quality of Air Circulation	Electrical: Power Failure	Power outage	Unacceptable level of toxins in air causing eye and skin irritation, lung and brain damage.	None	occassional	critical	2	Investigate design of exhaust electrical system
		Interference with Fan Blade Rotation	dirty, damaged during installation, poor design, damaged by foreign object	Fire, Unacceptable level of toxins in air causing eye and skin irritation, lung and brain damage.	Visual Inspection, Noise Heard	remote	critical	3	
Electric Oven	Cook Food	Electrical Failure	faulty wiring, crossed wiring, damaged insulation	potential fire hazard, failure to cook food	Visual Inspection, no heat buildup	occassional	critical	2	Establish Preventive Maintenance Program for oven
		Excessive dirt and Grime on oven, unit unable to cook effectively	no routine maintenance	potential fire hazard, failure to cook food	Visual Inspection	Probable	critical	1	Establish Preventive Maintenance Program for oven
Microwave	cook or reheat food	Electrical Failure	faulty wiring, crossed wiring, damaged insulation	potential fire hazard, failure to cook food	Visual inspection, no heat buildup	Remote	critical	3	

Item	Function	Failure Mode	Cause	Effect	Detection	Probability	Severity			Action
		Excessive dirt and Grime on oven, unit unable to cook effectively	no routine maintenance	potential fire hazard, failure to cook food	Visual Inspection	Probable	critical		1	Establish Preventive Maintenance Program for Microwave
Refrigerator	keep food cold	Electrical Failure	faulty wiring, crossed wiring, damaged insulation	potential fire hazard, failure to cook food	Visual Inspection	Probable	critical		1	Establish Preventive Maintenance Program for Refrigerator
Sink	wash food and hands	Employees Don't wash hands	no reminders in place	Unacceptable level of bacteria on hands.	None	Frequent	critical		1	Create Procedures for Handwashing
		Employees Don't wash food	no procedures in place for food washing	Unacceptable level of bacteria causing food borne illnesses.	Visual Inspection	occassional	critical		1	Create Procedures for food washing

Chapter 12

1. A. False The quality department serves as a resource. Those closest to the problem should solve it and reduce costs.

    B. True. Quality costs point out where waste exists.

    C. True. Defective products means that waste exists in the system.

2. Define Quality Costs

    Prevention costs are those costs that occur when a company is performing activities designed to prevent poor quality in products or services.

    Appraisal costs are the costs associated with measuring, evaluating, or auditing products or services to make sure that they conform to specifications or requirements.

    Failure costs occur when the completed product or service does not conform to customer requirements. Internal failure costs are those costs associated with product nonconformities or service failures found before the product is shipped or the service is provided to the customer. External failure costs are the costs that occur when a nonconforming product or service reaches the customer.

    Intangible costs, the hidden costs associated with providing a nonconforming product or service to a customer, involve the company's image.

3. Prevention costs are those costs that occur when a company is performing activities designed to prevent poor quality in products or services. Prevention costs focus on improving processes before errors occur. They can be found anywhere where process improvement is occurring.

4. Failure costs occur when the completed product or service does not conform to customer requirements. Internal failure costs are those costs associated with product nonconformities or service failures found before the product is shipped or the service is provided to the customer. External failure costs are the costs that occur when a nonconforming product or service reaches the customer. Failure costs come from situations where a defect has reached the end of a process or reached the customer. Any time something must be redone, a failure cost has occurred.

5. As more investment is made in preventing defects, the failure costs go down as do intangible costs. Appraisal costs decrease as quality improves.

6. As more investment is made in preventing defects, the failure costs go down as do intangible costs. A company's efforts should be focused on preventing defects. Effective organizations invest in prevention costs.

7. Graph

8. Quality costs can be used as a justification for actions taken to improve the product or service. Typically, investments in new equipment, materials, or facilities require the project sponsor to determine which projects will provide the greatest return on investment. These calculations traditionally include information on labor savings, production time savings, and ability to produce a greater variety of products with better quality. The "better quality" aspect of these calculations can be quantified by investigating the costs of quality, particularly the failure costs. It is important to determine the costs of in-process and incoming material inspection, sorting, repair, and scrap as well as the intangible costs associated with having a nonconforming product or service reach the customer. Making a decision with more complete quality information, such as product appraisal costs, can help determine the true profitability of a product or service.

9. The dollars should be invested in preventing defects from occurring in the first place.

10. Left to reader.

11. The further along the process that a failure is discovered, the more expensive it is to correct is true because the more of the product, service, process that is complete, the more things have

been done, actions taken. When the problem is discovered, there are more things to be redone or reworked. The effort to fix things is more costly.

12. Prevention of defects.

13. One key benefit of having, finding, or determining quality costs is knowing where waste is in the process.

14. Prevention of defects by identifying where waste occurs in the process.

15. Prevention costs: preventive maintenance, training, process improvement
    Appraisal costs: finished product inspection, incoming material inspection
    Failure costs (internal): finding defective cookies and candies during finished product inspection, rework, rewrap
    Failure costs (external): having the customer find defective candies or cookies
    Intangible costs: who would want to eat defective candy? Lost sales, loss of reputation

16. Friendly farmer used quality costs for decision making when they used warranty information to guide their improvement efforts.   The warranty information also served as their measure of performance: after making process improvements, did the number of warranty claims go down?

17. Quality costs
    a. External
    b. Internal
    c. Appraisal
    d. Prevention
    e. Internal
    f. External
    g. External
    h. Internal
    i. Prevention
    j. Prevention

Chapter 13

1. Product liability
   a. Airline A
   b. Estates of people who did not survive the crash
   c. The company could have made the effort to upgrade its navigation systems
2. Negligence occurs when the person manufacturing the product or providing the service has been careless or unreasonable.
3. Under strict liability, a manufacturer who makes and sells a defective product has committed a fault. A product is considered defectively made if it has a defect that causes it to be unreasonably dangerous and the defect is the reason for an injury.
4. The person was injured through no fault of his or her own; in other words, there was no contributory negligence.
5. The defendant is the person or company against whom a claim or suit is filed. Their role in a strict liability case is to show that the product had no defects at the time of manufacture.
6. Plaintiffs are the injured parties who file suit in a court of law. Their role in a strict liability case is to show that the product was defective and unreasonably dangerous and it caused harm.
7. Expert witnesses are chosen to inform the court about aspects of the accident, injury, product, or service. They must be technically competent in their field as evidenced by their degrees, years of experience, and professional activities. The behavior and credentials of an expert witness must be above reproach.
8. The court considers such factors as public knowledge of and ability to understand the danger, public use of the product, the advantage of the product to society, the negligence of the plaintiff and defendant.
9. Enact a statute of limitations for filing liability claims.

   Provide a release from liability for the original manufacturer if the item is modified or the safety devices have been removed or altered.

   Judge products according to state of the art at the time of manufacture or provision of service. Create a standard code of awards

   Reduce or eliminate punitive damages.

   Regulate attorney's fees.

   Institute comparative negligence judgments.

   Establish standards describing types of behavior that are grounds for punitive damages.

   Establish enhanced procedures for including scientific evidence of causes of injuries.

   Create nationwide standards for awards and litigation procedures.

   Accept compliance with government standards as a valid defense in lawsuits and a guarantee against punitive damages.

   Assess the legal fees of a successful defendant against the plaintiff.

10. – 18   Investigation left to reader

Chapter 14

1. Within a quality management system, the necessary ingredients exist to enable the organization's employees to identify, design, develop, produce, deliver, and support products or services that the customer wants. A quality management system is dynamic. It is able to adapt and change to meet the needs, requirements, and expectations of its customers.

2. Quality systems enable organizations to enhance their efficiency and effectiveness. They include process improvement as a key component of the system. Process improvement improves product and service quality.

3. Attributes: process improvement, management with a knowledge of variation, excellent communication throughout the organization, clear process ownership, clear processes and procedures, on-going training, preventive maintenance, process performance measures, customer focused organization, leadership, involvement of people, process approach, systems approach to management, continuous improvement, fact-based decision making, mutually beneficial supplier relationships, etc.

4. Left to the reader.

5. Any organization interested in improving its products and services with an eye to selling those products and services worldwide.

6. Left to reader.

7. Left to reader. See figure 14. 2.

8. TS 16949 is based on ISO 9001, the basic format is the same as shown in Figure 14.1. Additions to the document include: terms and definitions specific to the automotive industry, requirements related to engineering specifications and records retention, process efficiency expectations, product design skills and training related to human resources management, product realization, acceptance, and change control requirements, and customer designated special characteristics.

9. Left to reader.

10. The overall objective of the ISO 14000 Environmental Management Standard is to encourage environmental protection and the prevention of pollution while taking into account the economic needs of society. The standards can be followed by any organization interested in achieving and demonstrating sound environmental performance by limiting its negative impact on the environment. A company with an environmental management system like ISO 14000 is better able to meet its legal and policy requirements. Often, firms following ISO 14000 incur significant savings through better overall resource management and waste reduction. ISO 14000 provides the elements of an effective environmental management system. ISO 14000 is divided into two main classifications, Organization/Process-Oriented Standards and Product-Oriented Standards. A company complying with these standards is monitoring its processes and products to determine their effect on the environment. Within the two classifications, six topic areas are covered: Environmental Management Systems, Environmental Performance Evaluation, Environmental Auditing, Life-Cycle Assessment, Environmental Labeling, and Environmental Aspects in Product Standards. The ISO 14000 series of standards enables a company to improve environmental management voluntarily. The standards do not establish product or performance standards, establish mandates for emissions or pollutant levels, or specify test methods. The standards do not expand upon existing government regulations. ISO 14000 serves as a guide for environmentally conscious organizations seeking to lessen their impact on the environment.

11. Uniformity of output, reduced rework, fewer defective products, increased output, increased profit, lower average cost, fewer errors, less scarp, less rework, less downtime, less waste, increased job satisfaction, improved competitive position, more jobs, increased customer satisfaction.

12. Figure 14.2

13. In ISO 9000 a great deal of emphasis is placed on the need for excellent record keeping. In most cases, since the product has left the manufacturing facility or the service has been performed, only clearly kept records can serve as evidence of product or service quality. Sloppy or poorly maintained records give the impression of poor quality. High-quality records are easy to retrieve, legible, appropriate, accurate, and complete. Necessary records may originate internally or be produced externally. Customer or technical specifications and regulatory requirements are considered external records. Internally produced records include forms, reports, drawings, meeting minutes, problem-solving documentation, and process control charts. A high-quality documentation control system will contain records that are easily identified and used in the decision-making process.

14. **1.0 Leadership** The criteria in Section 1.0 are used to examine senior-level management's commitment to and involvement in process improvement. Company leaders are expected to develop and sustain a customer focus supported by visible actions and values on their part. This section also examines how the organization addresses its responsibilities to the public and exhibits good citizenship. Subcategories include senior leadership and governance and social responsibilities.

2.0 Strategic Planning To score well in this category, a company needs to have sound strategic objectives and action plans. The examiners also investigate how the company's strategic objectives and action plans are deployed and progress measured. Subcategories are strategy development and strategy deployment.

3.0 Customer and Market Focus The third category of the Baldrige Award criteria deals with the company's relationship with its customers. This category focuses on a company's knowledge of customer requirements, expectations, and preferences as well as marketplace competitiveness. Reviewers also determine if the company has put this knowledge to work in the improvement of their products, processes, systems, and services. Success in this category leads to improved customer acquisition, satisfaction, and retention. This category clarifies a company's commitment to its customers. The subcategories are customer and market knowledge, customer relationships, and satisfaction.

4.0 Measurement Analysis, and Knowledge Management The award recognizes that information is only useful when it is put to work to identify areas for improvement. This category investigates a company's use of information and performance measurement systems to encourage excellence. Performance information must be used to improve operational competitiveness. Competitive comparisons and benchmarking are encouraged. Subcategories include measurement, analysis, and improvement of organizational performance, and management of information, information technology, and knowledge.

5.0 Workforce Focus Within the human resource focus section, reviewers for the Baldrige Award are interested in a company's plans and actions that enable its workforce to perform to the fullest potential in alignment with the company's overall strategic objectives. Employee involvement, education, training, and recognition are considered in this category. A company's work environment receives careful scrutiny in an effort to determine how the company has built and maintains a work environment conducive to performance excellence as well as personal and organizational growth. Subcategories include workforce engagement and workforce environment.

6.0 Process Management Within this category, the company is judged on its process management abilities. Companies must provide details on their key business processes as they relate to customers, products, and service delivery. Subcategories are work systems design and work process management and improvement.

7.0 Results Ultimately, the purpose of being in business is to stay in business. This category examines a company's performance and improvement in several key business areas including customer satisfaction, product and service performance, financial and marketplace performance, human resources, and operational performance. Benchmarking is encouraged to see how the company compares with its competitors. Subcategories are product and service outcomes, customer-focused outcomes , financial and market outcomes, workforce focused outcomes, process effectiveness outcomes, and leadership outcomes.

15. Left to reader.

16. Table 14.1

17. Table 14.1, MBNQA focuses on the seven key areas that must be managed in order for an organization to be effective.

18. Six Sigma Breakthrough Strategy, which is essentially a highly focused system of problem-solving. Six Sigma's goal is to reach 3.4 defects per million opportunities over the long term. Six Sigma is about results, enhancing profitability through improved quality and efficiency. At the strategic business level, upper management must decide to implement Six Sigma. They set strategic business goals and metrics. At the operational process level, middle managers translate strategic business goals into process goals and measures. They also identify process problems and projects. At the project level, employees obtain green and black belt certifications while working on improvement projects throughout the organization. Six Sigma seeks to reduce the variability present in processes. Improvement projects are chosen based on their ability to contribute to the bottom line on a company's income statement. Projects should be connected to the strategic objectives and goals of the corporation.

19. Six Sigma seeks to reduce the variability present in processes. Improvement projects are chosen based on their ability to contribute to the bottom line on a company's income statement. Projects should be connected to the strategic objectives and goals of the corporation. Projects that do not directly tie to customer issues or financial results are often difficult to sell to management. Six Sigma projects are easy to identify. They seek out sources of waste such as overtime and warranty claims; investigate production backlogs or areas in need of more capacity; and focus on customer and environmental issues. With high volume products even small improvements can produce a significant impact on the financial statement.

20. Six Sigma tools include: problem solving, measures, process mapping, check sheets, Pareto analysis, cause and effect diagrams, scatter diagrams, frequency diagrams, histograms, statistics, sampling, x-bar and R charts, process capability studies, p, u, and c charts, root cause analysis, variation reduction, design of experiments, failure modes and effects analysis, etc.

21. Improvement projects are chosen based on their ability to contribute to the bottom line on a company's income statement. Projects should be connected to the strategic objectives and goals of the corporation. Projects that do not directly tie to customer issues or financial results are often difficult to sell to management. Six Sigma projects are easy to identify. They seek out sources of waste such as overtime and warranty claims; investigate production backlogs or areas in need of more capacity; and focus on customer and environmental issues. With high volume products even small improvements can produce a significant impact on the financial statement.

22. Figures 14.15 and 14.16.

Chapter 15

15.1 Steps involved in benchmarking. Determine the focus. Understand your organization. Determine what to measure. Determine whom to benchmark against. Benchmark. Improve performance.

15.2 The primary benefit of benchmarking is the knowledge gained about where a company stands when compared against standards set by their customers, themselves, or national certification or award requirements. With this knowledge, a company can develop strategies for meeting their own continuous improvement goals. The benchmarking experience will identify assets within the company as well as opportunities for improvement. Most quality-assurance certifications involve discovering how the company is currently performing, strengthening the weaknesses, and then verifying compliance with the certification standards. Since a benchmarking assessment provides an understanding of how the company is performing, it is a valuable tool to use throughout the certification process.

15.3 Left to reader.

15.4 Steps involved in benchmarking. Determine the focus. Understand your organization. Determine what to measure. Determine whom to benchmark against. Benchmark. Improve performance. They can benchmark other banks naturally, however, they should consider any organization that handles money, like a credit card bill processing company.

15.5 Steps involved in benchmarking. Determine the focus. WP and Me should determine the key areas of the award and focus their benchmarking there. Understand your organization. WP and Me should determine their key processes and how they operate. They should map how information flows through their organization. Determine what to measure. They should relate what they measure to the compliance document requirements. Determine whom to benchmark against. They should benchmark against first in field organizations. Benchmark. Improve performance. They should use the information they gain to make positive changes for their organization.

15.6 a. continuous improvement benchmark assessment
b. Steps involved in benchmarking. Determine the focus. The bank should determine the key areas that they want to improve and focus their benchmarking there. Understand your organization. The bank should determine their key processes and how they operate. They should map how information flows through their organization. Determine what to measure. They should relate what they measure to their key process input and output variables. Determine whom to benchmark against. They should benchmark against first in field organizations. Benchmark. Improve performance. They should use the information they gain to make positive changes for their organization.

15.7

1. *Plan:* To begin, those planning the audit need to identify its purpose or objective. A statement of purpose clarifies the focus of the audit. Following this, planners will need to identify the who, what, where, when, why, and how related to the audit. Who is to be audited? Who is to perform the audit? What does this audit hope to accomplish? Is the audit to judge conformance to standards? If so, what are the critical standards? What are the

performance measures? When and where the audit will be conducted must be set. Those about to be audited should be informed by an individual in a position of authority. Clear statements of the reasons behind the audit (why), the performance measures (what), and the procedures (how) should be given to those being audited. An audit is a valuable working document for improvement. It is important to determine how the results will be used and who will have access to the results before the auditing process begins.

2. *Do:* Using the information clarified in the planning phase, the audit is conducted. Often an introductory meeting is held by the participants to discuss the scope, objectives, schedule, and paperwork considerations. After the opening meeting, examiners begin the process of reviewing the process, product, or system under study. Auditors may require access to information concerning quality systems, equipment operation procedures, preventive maintenance records, inspection histories, or planning documents. Auditors may conduct interviews with those involved in the process of providing a product or service. Any and all information related to the area under study is critical for the success of the audit. Organizations conducting audits may ask questions like those provided in Figure 15.4. To make an audit more successful consider using these techniques. Begin by encouraging those being audited to be part of the audit team. If they are involved, they will emerge with a clearer understanding of the gap between what was expected and what was found. It also helps to begin the audit by asking general open-ended questions. Once the auditor has a grasp of the big picture, these can be followed by more concise questions used for clarification. Naturally, a good auditor is also a good listener. Auditors should do significantly more listening than talking in order to find out how things are really operating in a department.

3. *Study:* Audits provide information about the participant's strengths, weaknesses, and areas for improvement. Upon receipt, the auditor's report is read by the participants in the audit. During this phase of the audit cycle, they respond to the report and develop an action plan based on the recommendations of the auditors. This action plan should specify the steps and time frame involved in dealing with the issues raised by the audit.

4. *Act:* Once adopted, the action plan becomes the focus of the improvement activities related to the audited area. Auditors and company administrators should follow up at predetermined intervals to evaluate the status of the continuous improvement action plan. This ensures that the recommendations and conclusions reached by the auditors, and supported by an action plan, assist the company in reaching its continuous improvement goals.

15.8   Audits are designed to appraise the activities, practices, records, and policies of an organization to determine the company's ability to meet or exceed a standard. The benefits an organization receives include a better understanding of the organization's current status, and understanding of where improvements are needed, and knowledge with which to manage the organization.

15.9   Left to the reader.

15.10 Five questions: How helpful was the clerk in finding an item? How many of the items on my list was I able to find easily? Where the prices of the items clearly marked? Did the prices charged for the item match the listed prices? Was the store clean? Was the store layout arranged in a way that made sense? Etc. Good questions capture the customer's experience, their stated and unstated needs, their subjective or technically operational requirements, and their conscious or merely sensed expectations. These questions can help determine the ability of the store to meet customer expectations, needs, and requirements.

15.11   Audits need to be carefully planned in order to make sure that the information gathered is pertinent and that the information can be used to make improvements to company performance. *Plan:* To begin, those planning the audit need to identify its purpose or objective. A statement of purpose clarifies the focus of the audit. Following this, planners will need to identify the who, what, where, when, why, and how related to the audit. Who is to be audited? Who is to perform the audit? What does this audit hope to accomplish? Is the audit to judge conformance to standards? If so, what are the critical standards? What are the performance measures? When and where the audit will be conducted must be set. Those about to be audited should be informed by an individual in a position of authority. Clear statements of the reasons behind the audit (why), the performance measures (what), and the procedures (how) should be given to those being audited. An audit is a valuable working document for improvement. It is important to determine how the results will be used and who will have access to the results before the auditing process begins.

15.12   During the review process, auditors document their findings. These findings are presented in a general summary at a meeting of the participants. Within a short period of time, perhaps 10 to 20 days, the auditors will prepare a written report that documents their findings, conclusions, and recommendations. The report should be detailed enough to provide a clear picture of the situation. This will help those being audited understand what was found versus what was required. The report should quantify the costs associated with gaps in performance, thus tying their findings to real consequences. The reports should not be entirely negative either. Auditors should also point out specific areas where the organization is performing well.